The "Tricks of the Trade" Guide to

HOME RENOVATION

The "Tricks of the Trade" Guide to

HOME RENOVATION

PETER JONES

NEW CENTURY PUBLISHERS, INC.

BOOK DESIGN: Jacques Chazaud

ILLUSTRATIONS: Albert Pfeiffer, Jr.
                    Ken Rice
                    Mark Richards
                    Gary Tong

The Publisher believes that the material contained herein is accurate, but disclaims all responsibility in connection with its use or misuse.

Printing Code

11   12   13   14   15   16

Library of Congress Catalog Card Number: 81-83527

ISBN 0-8329-0221-7

Printed in United States of America

Contents

Introduction:
Why Renovate?

THE MILLIONS OF HOMEOWNERS in America divide into two distinct groups. The preference of one group is to buy and dwell in only a modern construction, on the premise that a new building requires no maintenance, no renovation, no work whatsoever. But there are almost as many people who refuse to consider living in anything but an older home. To these millions, old houses are a part of the collective memory of man—receptacles of forgotten joys and sadnesses that somehow linger in the vacant rooms and dark hallways. They provide constant reminders that other people have lived there at different times and under different circumstances. And somehow, dwelling in an old house lets the present owners share those past lives.

There is another charm about old houses, and that is that they were literally made by the hand of man. They were seldom mass-produced on the scale that homes are constructed today, and to those who live in them, there is something reassuring about floors that are now not quite level and walls that have shifted a little out of plumb. Older houses are frequently examples of profound craftsmanship and detail that cannot be duplicated in our modern times—at least not by professionals, who may have the skills but not the time to do the painstaking work necessary.

Whether you belong to the old- or the new-house group of homeowners, the plain fact of ownership is that every residence must be annually attended to. The list of maladies that can occur, even to a new house, is almost endless: The plumbing can develop leaks. Electrical wiring for all of the modern household appliances may become inadequate. The cellar can flood. Heating bills continue to rise. And so forth.

Many owners taking title to a house find themselves paralyzed by the "leave it alone" syndrome, which can be defined as an unwillingness to disturb any surface in order to solve a mechanical problem that may lurk underneath. In its mildest form, "leave it aloneness" leads to extra expenses. At its severest, it can allow trouble to go unabated until a once minor problem reaches disaster proportions.

The cause of the "leave it alone" plague is an acute case of fear: fear of making a mess, fear of making holes where none existed before, fear of the inability to put everything back in order so that it will appear that nothing was ever wrong.

The way a great many people cope with this rabid homeowner's disease is to hire outsiders to do the work. Chances are that any outsider who comes bearing the label of "professional" is assumed to be capable of doing a better job than the homeowner who stands there in his domain inert from inactivity. But it is not true that every plumber or every electrician can do all of the job he is hired to do better than the man who hires him. The only real advantage an outside "expert" has is that he is not emotionally involved with the house in which he is hired to work. To him, your precious kingdom is just another work site. If he needs to open up a wall to see what is going on inside, he does not hesitate to start banging large holes in the structure—and he will proceed with a ruthlessness that can send shivers down the spine of the sturdiest houseowner alive. Very often, the actual repairs to an older home are quite simple once the wall, ceiling, or floor is open. In fact, the repairs are usually well within the capabilities of any home craftsman.

There is a distinction, however, between making a few holes to get at the plumbing or electrical wiring and the wholesale removal of material from the house. Removal of very much of anything is likely to change the fabric of the house, and that should be undertaken only after considerable thought and study. Many a home has been forever damaged by a new owner's zeal to make "improvements"—modifications that have resulted in the destruction of precious details or the irreparable alteration of the proportions of the building. By the same token, many an old house has been adapted to the needs of modern living by judicious structural change. So, the most sensible attitude to assume whenever considering major structural changes is to retain a deep respect for the intent of the structure's original builders.

In our modern society, which puts a premium on sheer volume and production, there is still a profound satisfaction in taking all of the time necessary to do a home renovation in the very best possible way. While renovating a house can be a long and painful process, it is also one of the most creative and rewarding of all experiences. To those who love the houses they live in and find a personal joy in reviving them and keeping them as close as possible to their original vibrant condition, renovating any house, be it old or new, is really nothing more than a state of mind.

Many of the suggestions and tips provided in this book pertain specifically to old houses, to buildings that were constructed with rough-hewn beams, lath and plaster walls, and 100-year-old brick. But the solutions to many of the problems discussed here are equally applicable to any modern home. Thus, when a floor begins to sag, it is shored up in exactly the same manner, whether the boards are 75 years old or three months young.

Still, this is not a standard home-repair book. It is written to be helpful to anyone, whether he or she is a newcomer to the art of home repair or a lifelong carpenter. It's assumed only that you have a very basic familiarity with tools and how to use them. For the most part, the text outlines the easiest ways to proceed in many areas of home renovation, from knocking down a wall to installing a bathtub or adding a dormer. Much of the information relies on the insider's point of view—in fact, that is where this book begins. The tips on home renovation presented here are tricks of the trade—ins and outs and professional "secrets" that most renovators guard from amateur handymen. The suggestions and approaches have been gleaned from a number of "old pros," some of them workmen who learned their craftsmanship in other countries in bygone years, others who developed their own techniques and successful procedures from many hours of wrestling with modern structures, materials, and tools. And still other hints come from the personal experience of amateurs who, in the course of renovating their homes, have developed unique approaches that make the work easier.

This is a book of footnotes to home renovation, then, a collection of the small details that will go a long way in making your home look the way you want it to—and keeping it that way.

1. Before You Renovate

BEFORE YOU RENOVATE a house, you have to buy it. Before you buy any house, you should have a complete engineer's inspection report. If you were too thrifty to spend the $135 or so for a thorough inspection report made by a competent professional before you moved into the home you want to rehabilitate, spend the money now—it could save you thousands of dollars in renovation costs.

The inspection report is a marvel of negative statements about the house you live in or are thinking about buying. If the house happens to be an old one, there is no way it is going to meet the standards of perfection set forth by the inspector on the checklist he has anchored to his clipboard. Engineers' inspection reports have prevented many an old house from being sold because they are designed to ferret out all of the major and minor problems in any building, from inadequate wiring to dangerously old (and therefore weak) plumbing, leaky roofs, wonky boilers, and "excessively crowded" garages. The inspectors themselves, by the way, happen to be knowledgeable, and usually very nice people. It's just that you are paying them to tell you the truth about the house, and sometimes the truth is ugly.

The inspection report is also a guide to renovation. It lists at least 90 percent and maybe all of the problems with your building. In other words, it tells you what has to be renovated for optimum safety, security, and operation of the building. You may want to make a lot of other changes that have to do with the arrangement of your living space and how it looks, but the engineer's inspection report warns you about the state of the plumbing, wiring, and heating systems, as well as the condition of the roof, the gutter system, the exterior, and the basement. Maybe the subject of crumbling lintels and roofs bores you when all you want to do is put in a new kitchen, but all of the systems that make up the functional aspects of your house happen to be the most expensive changes you will make (if you have to make them), and deficiencies in any of them must be overcome before you even consider decorating a single room.

Suppose, for example, you move into your new home and follow the worldwide human instinct to open a can of paint and attack those faded walls and dirty ceilings. You diligently refurbish the walls, the ceilings, and the floors, move in the family heirlooms, and complete your renovation just in time for the hot water supply lines running up inside the walls to burst—while you're away for the weekend. A ruptured pipe can pour thousands of gallons of water into the living room and basement by the time you get home. The worst part about the mess is that the inspection report you didn't get, or didn't bother to read carefully, or ignored, probably warned you that the plumbing system was 50-year-old galvanized steel and showed signs of not being able to withstand the water rushing through it under 60 pounds of pressure. Don't invite disaster: invest in an engineer's inspection report and use it to your advantage.

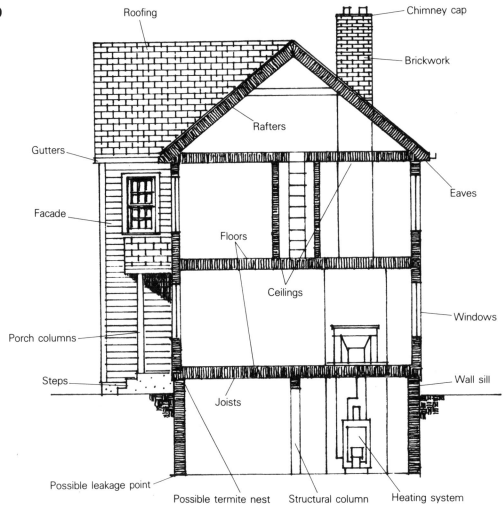

Roofing · Chimney cap · Brickwork · Rafters · Gutters · Eaves · Facade · Floors · Ceilings · Windows · Porch columns · Steps · Wall sill · Joists · Possible leakage point · Possible termite nest · Structural column · Heating system

Some of the more important areas in a house that are closely checked and evaluated during an engineer's inspection report

THE BASIC ELEMENTS OF RENOVATION

The basic steps in renovating any house are very simple. To avoid disaster and unnecessary expense, it's best to follow these steps in the order listed:

1. Take care of all mechanical systems throughout the house. This means that every por-

tion of the plumbing, electrical, heating, air conditioning, and ventilation systems must be upgraded to meet modern living needs. You may be able to use the existing systems, but they might be outdated and require some expansion or upgrading. Electrical systems, particularly in any house built before 1960, may not be adequate to handle all of the modern appliances in your household.

You can pretty much rely on your inspection report to point out most of the deficiencies in your mechanical systems, but it is probably worth a few extra dollars to call in several specialists, one to look at each system. They can also provide an estimate of what it will cost to have them make the necessary repairs or upgrades to the system. With that in hand you can evaluate, in terms of your own capabilities and pocketbook, whether or not you want to do the work yourself.

2. Make a complete floor plan of the room arrangements you want to alter. *Complete.* Don't just sketch the kitchen and then start knocking down the walls. Measure and draw each of the areas to be affected. An extra couple of hours spent at this stage may save you thousands of dollars and immeasurable headache and heartache later.

3. Locate and price all of the equipment you plan to install in the house: kitchen cabinets, stall showers, tubs, sinks, toilets, refrigerators, dishwashers, clothes washers and dryers—anything made by an outside manufacturer that has a prescribed size and power or water requirements. You need to evaluate the make and model of each piece of equipment, and whether you have provided enough space for it in the room where you plan to put it. You must also make allowances for bringing power or water to your equipment, if that is what it needs to operate. Only after you've done careful planning should you go ahead and buy the equipment you need.

4. Now you can consider the decorating, the color paint you will need and how much of it, wallpaper, flooring, and so on, and what has to be done to achieve the final look of each room. It helps if you make a list of tasks to be done in each room.

How About the Outside?

In most instances, renovation of the outside of a house is not a primary consideration—at least not in making the house functional and livable. It may be a personal concern. It may be a concern of the neighborhood, or the block where the house stands, particularly if the house hasn't been painted for fifteen years and stands out as

an eyesore. There may be some dangers involved—if, for example, the facade has loose stonework or broken stoop steps. Most of all, there may be a personal pride lurking in your soul that drives you to repair the front of the building before you do anything else. That's your privilege. It is usually not necessary, but you can certainly work from the outside in, if you wish.

Even if you are not attending to the facade first, make certain that the roof is watertight, and that the gutters and leaders are performing their function of carrying water away from the building. Water runoff has a considerable amount to do with wet basements, so if you have a problem with a flooding cellar after heavy rains, making the gutters and leaders work properly may provide the solution.

The approaches to installing new mechanical systems or upgrading your existing ones are discussed in Chapter 2. Even as these systems are being upgraded, it is important to develop a full plan for your entire renovation. One of the reasons you need a complete plan is economics, but it is just as important that you also have a full knowledge of exactly what you have to work with. It is only through the development of a well-thought-out plan that you can be sure all of the space you need will be provided. You can run into some serious problems, for example, if you decide to create a new bathroom and forget to allow enough space for the door to swing into the room, or if you forget to allow enough closets in a bedroom.

BUILDING CODES

In most locales, communities demand that you show the municipal building department a detailed plan of any major alterations and additions you plan to make to any structure. There are some variations from community to community, but generally, any major renovation requires a building permit, which may call for one or two inspections by a certified inspector employed by the municipality. The purpose of all this is so that your local governmental agency is assured that all major alterations to your building meet the community's standards for both health and safety.

There is a great deal to be said in favor of building codes and building inspectors. In terms of practical advice they can offer during your renovation, codes and inspectors are more often valuable than not. Building codes are particularly concerned with structural soundness, adequate daylight and ventilation, provisions for emergency fire exits, safety in the electrical wiring, and the impossibility of crossover between the water supply lines and the drain-waste-vent system. If the federal government is providing any of the money for your renovation, you will also have to show some explicit drawings of how you intend to meet the fed's own requirements.

You can measure the rooms you plan to renovate and make all of the drawings yourself, then take them to your local building department and usher them through their reviews, make the changes they require, and eventually get a building permit. In typical small towns, most suburbs, and even some cities, the process is not terribly time consuming or even frustrating. In a big city, encumbered by unwieldy bureaucracy and complicated, often antiquated building codes, months can pass before you may even figure out how to get a building permit, let alone acquire one. It is worth the small fee an architect or some contractors will charge you to do the drawings and obtain a permit on your behalf.

Actually, if you are contemplating major structural changes in any building, it pays to hire an architect on an hourly basis for a number of economic reasons. Architects are not infallible, but they spend their business lives figuring out ways of utilizing space. They have entire shelvesful of catalogs showing equipment they can put into the spaces they design. They know all kinds of tricks for saving money. Better still, most architects can design a space to be built either by professionals or amateurs. And if you have hired one on an hourly basis, he will even come around from time to time and give you advice as the work progresses.

THE WORKING PLAN

No matter how large or small a renovation you intend to make, you will need some sort of working drawing so that you know exactly where every wall, door, and window is to be placed. You can also use the drawing to accurately estimate the materials you will have to buy, which in turn will allow you to reckon the total cost of the renovation before you begin any work.

The working plan need not be elaborate, only accurate. It does not have to win any art critic's awards, either, but it must contain specific information and, for your own sake, it ought to be done to some sort of scale. The easiest way of achieving that scale is to buy a pad of ruled graph paper which is divided into ¼" squares. By assuming each square equals 1 foot, you can arrive at a pretty readable layout without any problems at all. Of course, you can allocate the squares to equal any real distance you wish.

Your working drawing should include the following features and pieces of information. You can use some of the standard symbols shown in Chart A, but the meaning of those symbols, along with the scale of the drawing ought to be listed somewhere in a corner of your plan.

1. The existing walls that will remain during the renovation, and those that will be removed.

2. All new walls and partitions to be built. Each of these should be noted as to the types of materials used to construct them.

3. Enough dimensions to accurately locate all of the new work to be done in relation to the existing walls and partitions. You don't have to measure out every little quarter-inch, just get the nearly accurate distances down and mark them plus or minus, so that you know when you get to that portion of the job that you will have to make some minor adjustments.

4. All new door and window openings and their dimensions. Include the width of each door and the direction in which it will swing, because

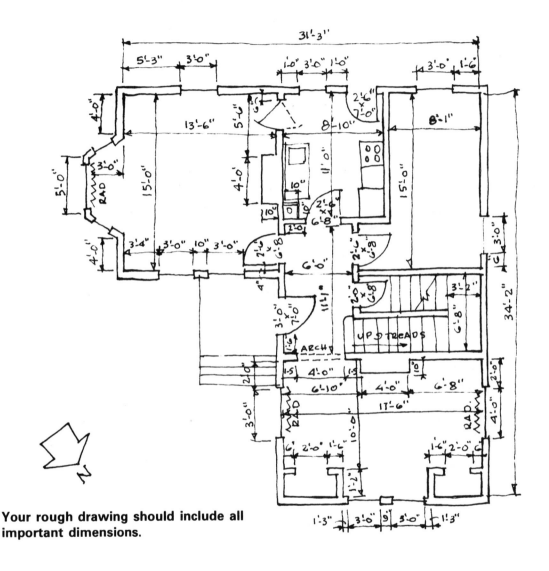

Your rough drawing should include all important dimensions.

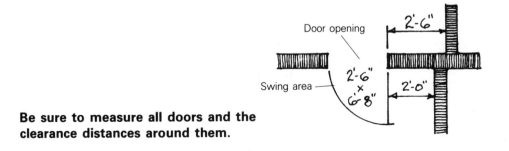

Door opening

Swing area

Be sure to measure all doors and the clearance distances around them.

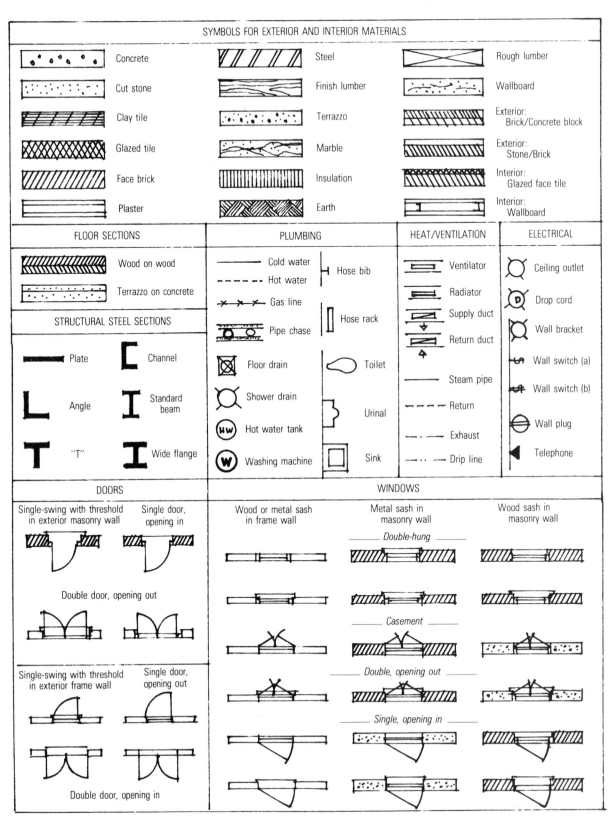

CHART A: Symbols used in architectural drawings

you may find that it hits another door, or that it can't be opened completely unless you put a notch in it—say, to get past the lip of a toilet seat.

5. The position of all new electrical fixtures, plumbing lines, old and new radiators, and ducts.

MEASURING FOR YOUR WORKING PLAN

In order to work up a plan for any renovation you have to measure the existing space, and note its dimensions. It is handy to have a clipboard loaded with 8½" × 11" ruled paper or graph paper, a yardstick or folding carpenter's rule (for measuring vertical areas), and a measuring tape, preferably one that is 25 or 50 feet long. You also ought to have a sharp pencil with a good eraser.

Before you measure anything, make a rough sketch of the areas to be renovated, including the approximate proportions of the rooms and the positions of the doors and windows in each wall. You want to show all of the recesses and projections, and make them as large as you can on the piece of paper you are using, so there will be plenty of space for your measurement notations.

While accuracy is important in all of your measurements, you can keep them to the nearest half-inch on your plan. Thus, 5 feet-6¼" would be put down as 5' 6", while 7 feet-8⅝" becomes 7' 8½". Only in unusual situations is it necessary to use any fraction less than a half-inch.

Also, be sure you make your measurements from the right place—that is, from wall surface to wall surface, or from floor to ceiling, *not* from the baseboards, molding, or trim, or from the floor to the crown molding around the edge of the ceiling.

MEASUREMENT CHECKLIST

1. Measure the overall length, width, and height of the space. If you are including more than one room in your plan, still make the overall measurements first, and mark them on your sketch. The overall measurements are easy to forget and difficult to work out if you only have the

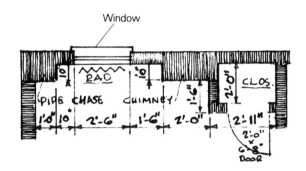

Show all recesses and projections in your sketches. Take overall measurements of each wall and use them to verify the individual distances.

The only way you can really judge the squareness of a room is to make diagonal measurements.

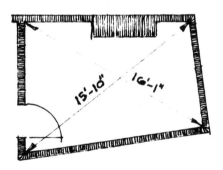

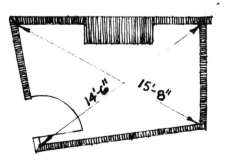

room measurements, which would have to be added up along with the exact thicknesses of the partitions and walls.

2. Measure each room. First take down the overall length, width, and height. Then measure the position of each projection, alcove, window, and door. When you get finished inching your way along a wall, you can add up all the little distances and double-check them against the overall lengths.

When you are measuring most spaces, you really only need to take the measurements necessary to locate all of the major features of the room. Doors, for example, normally require measurement only of their height and width, plus the distance to the nearest wall.

3. If you have any suspicions that a room you are measuring is not square, take a few diagonal measurements. If a room is truly square or rectangular, the diagonal distances between any two opposite corners will be identical. It is surprising how often rooms that are apparently square turn out to have walls that are not 90°. An irregular room can affect the swing on doors and the direction that new walls will take, as well as the positions of windows, so it's best to know in advance just how regular the space you are renovating really is.

4. If your renovation will include tampering with the existing windows and doors in any way, make a separate profile sketch of the units, known as a jamb section. If you are enlarging or removing a door or window, you need to know the dimensions of the trim, which you will be re-

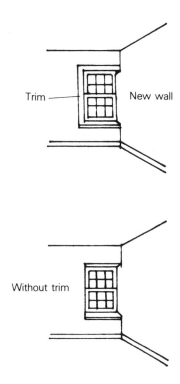

Trim   New wall

Without trim

You want to be careful about symmetry. The trim around a window, for example, might best be left off if a new wall comes so close to the opening that part of the molding is lost.

moving, but may want to replace around your new units. Similarly, if a partition wall is to come close to the trim around a door or window, you will need to know how much space you have for relating the door and window trim to the wall.

5. Heights are often neglected when people measure the rooms they intend to renovate. The floor-to-ceiling measurements is usually taken, but the distance from the floor to the bottom of windows, or the distance from the top of a door or window to the ceiling, is sometimes forgotten. Other heights to remember are the amount of clearance under stairways, ducts, pipes, or sloping ceilings such as you might find in an attic.

A profile drawing of windows and doors can be very helpful.

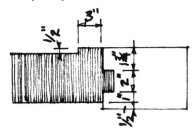

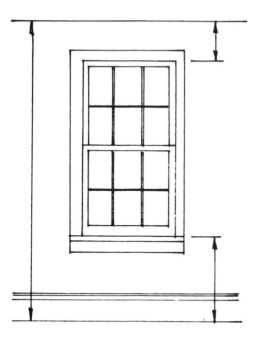

Don't forget to measure the distances from the floor to the bottom of a window, and from the window to the ceiling.

6. Stairways should be carefully drawn on your sketch, and width as well as length must be noted. Also count the number of treads, and measure the height of the risers.

7. Check all elements that represent an expense if they must be moved, such as ductwork, plumbing, risers, stacks, or chimney breasts. Measure them and accurately place them on the sketch. You may discover that some of the partition walls are more than the standard 5" or 6" thick. If they are unusually thick, you can be pretty certain they are hiding plumbing or gas pipes, or they may be (or once have been) used to contain pocket sliding doors, and are therefore hollow. Also note which walls are load-bearing—that is, which ones are holding up the house and cannot be tampered with. If you blithely take down a load-bearing wall, the rest of the house is very likely to come with it.

Drawing a Working Plan

If you have to submit your working drawings to the local buildings department for approval, use a drawing board, T-square, triangle, compass, and an H or 2H pencil, and draw a first-rate plan on a medium-grade tracing paper. If you are making the plans for yourself and they do not have to pass muster anywhere, you can develop perfectly accurate and very workable drawings using a ruler, pencil, and a pad of graph paper. Essentially, all you are doing is reproducing your rough sketch in a formal, right-angled drawing that includes all of the important dimensions and information you will need in order to get on with the actual work of renovating your house. The plan must include the position of all the new walls, partitions, windows, doors, and other necessary architectural features.

ARRANGING THE ROOMS

The spaces in a house can be divided into four main areas: living, utility, storage, and circulation. Living rooms, dining rooms, family rooms, and bedrooms all come under the heading of living space, and they should always be given the largest floor space possible. Generally, they need better access to daylight and views.

An unusually thick wall may hold large plumbing pipes or old ductwork, or might have been used to contain a pocket sliding door.

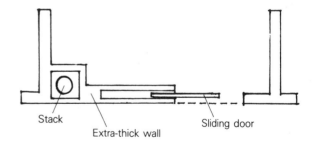

Stack   Sliding door

Extra-thick wall

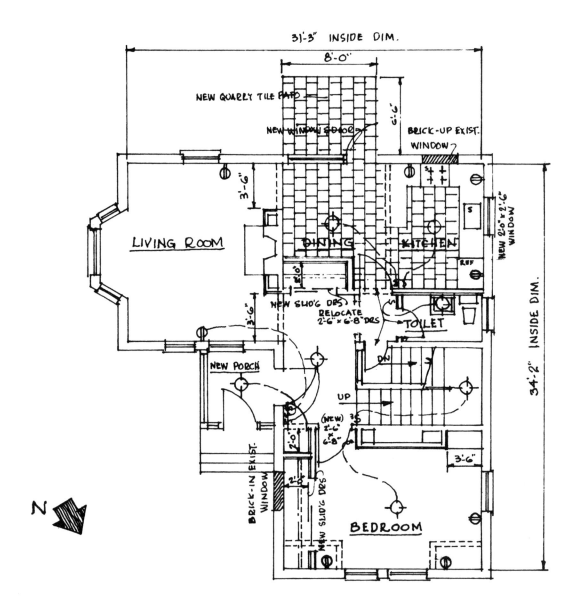

31'-3" INSIDE DIM.

8'-0"

NEW QUARRY TILE PATIO

NEW WINDOW & DOOR

6'-6"

BRICK-UP EXIST. WINDOW

LIVING ROOM

3'-6"

DINING   KITCHEN

NEW 2'0" x 2'-6" WINDOW

REF.

3'-6"

NEW SL40'G DRS.
RELOCATE 2'-6" x 6'-8" DRS

34'-2" INSIDE DIM.

TOILET

NEW PORCH

DN

UP

(NEW)
2'-6"
x
6'-8"

3'-6"

BRICK-IN EXIST. WINDOW

2'-0"

2'-6"

NEW SLID'G DRS

N

BEDROOM

Formal drawings should be done neatly with a straightedge, and should include only the essential measurements.

Kitchens, utility rooms, and bathrooms are classified as utility areas. They do not always have to have windows, but they should have some form of ventilation. In fact, in urban homes—particularly row houses that abut each other and have windows only in their front and back walls—the utility spaces are often located in the center of the building, in which case some form of mechanical ventilation is required by the municipality building code. Which means you have to allow both the money and space to install ventilation ducts from all interior rooms to the outside.

Storage space is, of course, all manner of closets, which should be numerous as well as conveniently located. No one ever has enough closets. Circulation space—that is, stairways and halls—should be accessible, and kept to a minimum both in number and dimension.

All of the rooms in your home can be any size you wish to make them, although their specific dimensions will be guided not only by their orientation to the outside world and to each other, but by the economy of creating them, along with the amount of overall space you have to work with. As a general guideline, the federal government has published some minimum suggested dimensions for healthy occupancy:

SPACE	MINIMUM DIMENSIONS
Living room	10′ × 10′
Dining room	7′8″ × 7′8″
Kitchen	5′4″ × 5′4″
Kitchenette	3′6″ × 3′6″
Single bedroom	7′ × 7′
Double bedroom	8′8″ × 8′8″

Adjacent Rooms

The living-space category, encompassing the living room, dining room, family room, and bedrooms, can be further classified according to the human functions of eating, sleeping, and living. The functions of living and eating are not mutually exclusive, so it is not unusual to group a living and dining room next to one other. The two rooms can, in fact, be part of the same area, providing a sense of spaciousness, or they can be separated by a partition or wall.

Sleeping rooms are for the separate function of sleeping, and they should be clustered somewhere away from the living space to provide a semblance of, if not total, privacy. Although many modern apartments have their bedrooms opening from a living room, you should try to avoid the arrangement if at all possible. Bedrooms, however, can—even should—be adjacent to a bathroom, again for the sake of privacy as well as convenience. It should not be necessary, for example, to cross a living or dining room from a bedroom to reach the nearest bathroom.

Many old homes were built in an era when households included a staff. Consequently, you will often find the kitchen is considerably removed from the dining room, and even from the rest of the house. Modern families moving into an old home invariably find that some of the renovation they must do is to bring the kitchen nearer, and preferably adjacent to, the dining room.

While the living-dining-kitchen/bedrooms-bathroom division of the major spaces in a home is ideal, economics can play havoc with the actual arrangement. Plumbing, for example, can be a very expensive proposition, particularly if a new or secondary soil stack must be installed. The cost of running a new soil stack from the house drain in the cellar up three floors to service one new bathroom is outrageous (reckon $2,000 to $5,000 for the rough plumbing alone). In the interest of economics, since the stack and its attendant piping systems must be installed, it is more reasonable to connect the lines for a second bathroom or the kitchen to the same stack. But the cost of the plumbing is guiding the major decisions as to where you locate your bathroom and the kitchen. And with the kitchen situated, placement of the dining room and living room is affected as well.

All of the possibilities and their costs must be carefully weighed, and solutions to the problems they present must be solved on paper, *before* you begin any renovation. If they are not resolved before you start, they will have to be reckoned with after work is in progress, and at that point their solutions may come at an inordinately high cost in time, labor, and money.

PLAN, PLAN, PLAN

Most people, when they move into a new home, are intent on some form of renovation—if only painting the walls and scraping the floors. It cannot be emphasized too much that no matter how little or extensive your rehabilitation plans may be, the work should not begin until you have a complete plan of action. Every room should be examined inside and out, and each renovation that you think you will want to make should be written down and allocated a priority. That priority should be based on living needs as well as economics, and should be integrated with all of the other projects you have in mind. Only when you have organized all of the changes you want to make can you begin to judge their magnitude. If a new kitchen must be installed in addition to a second-floor bathroom, it's best if you determine their physical relationship and place them in proximity to the plumbing lines needed to make either room functional. If the third-floor sitting room is to be divided into a sleeping and playing space for children, you may have to knock down or build some walls, but you may also have to bring more electricity up to the third floor. That means some of the walls in the first two floors will have to be opened up. But if that is to be done, it is less expensive to have the electricians do a wiring job throughout the house when they are there, rather than keep asking them back every few months. Nevertheless, you can't ask an electrician, or even yourself, to run 220-volt power lines for air conditioners, electric ranges, and clothes dryers until you know where those appliances will be placed.

Unless all you are doing is painting and floor polishing, there has to be an organized plan that includes every renovation you intend to make at present and in the foreseeable future. From that plan you can pretty accurately estimate where the mechanical systems—the plumbing, electricity, ventilation, and heating lines—will run.

The mechanical systems are best installed before the real renovation work begins, primarily because plumbing, heating, and electrical systems nearly always require the opening up of walls, floors, and ceilings. That is always a messy procedure. But to save costs as well as time (which is money), the mechanical experts should be invited to do their work as soon after any necessary demolition is completed.

Given all of the considerations—the types of rooms and their physical relationship to each other, the mechanical requirements of your renovation, and the initial drawings you have made of the existing spaces—an overall renovation plan can then be devised. In formulating that plan, it might be helpful to ask yourself several questions about the general layout of your house as you envision it will be:

1. Which rooms need the most daylight, and will they get it by the time your renovation is complete?

2. Will the rooms that need direct sunlight get it?

3. Which side of the house is best for the living room? Does it have to face the noisy street? Or are you planning to have a beautiful garden in the backyard, which would be more gracious to look at than a main thoroughfare?

4. Can the living room be located without taking down too many structural walls?

5. Will you be able to go from the bedrooms to the bath without entering a living area?

6. Are there toilet facilities near the living area, so that people don't have to pass too many bedrooms on the way to the bathroom?

7. Is the dining area convenient to the kitchen?

8. Are there enough plumbing stacks, or do you need to add or subtract one? The fewer the better.

9. Are the rooms proportionally large enough for their intended use?

10. Do halls and stairways take away too much space from the living areas?

2. The Mechanical Lifelines

CRITICAL TO the uninterrupted functioning of any house are its mechanical systems' supply lines, which connect the building to the outside world. Two of the mechanical systems derive their sources of supply from the community beyond the house itself: electricity is almost always brought to the house by local-utility-company power lines; municipal water is similarly provided for most houses, and whatever water is not used is sent back under the streets to be disposed of through the city's sewage system. There are, of course, exceptions to the rule when fresh water comes from a well and sewage is expelled in a disposal field or septic tank. (In some isolated cases, homeowners provide all or most of their own electrical needs via a windmill or hydrogenerator.) But insofar as renovating a house is concerned, the source of electrical power or water makes no difference whatsoever.

The third mechanical system in most houses is the heating system. As a system contained entirely within the building, it includes a furnace, perhaps a boiler, and ducts or pipes that extend to each of the rooms to be heated. The furnace may be designed to heat water to 180°F. to supply hot water radiators in each room. Or the boiler may heat the water until it turns into steam, which again is sent to a series of radiators. A third possibility is that the furnace heats air, which is then blown through ducts that go all over the house.

How electricity gets to your house

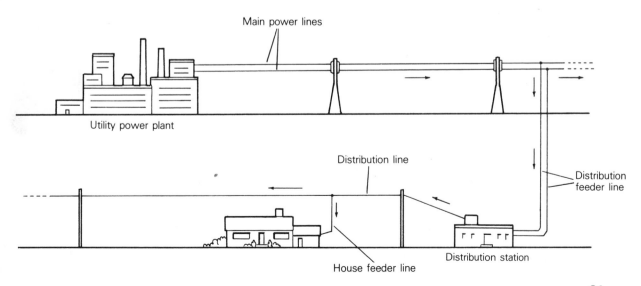

Main power lines

Utility power plant

Distribution line

Distribution feeder line

House feeder line

Distribution station

Furnaces can be oil-fired, electrically powered, or natural gas–fired. If oil is the source of fuel, it is usually stored in a tank in the cellar or buried in the ground just outside the house. Either way, the tank is periodically filled by a home-heating-oil company. If natural gas is used, it is normally piped into the house by a gas utility company serving the entire community. Electricity, of course, also comes from an outside source.

So the lifelines that make a building function properly all connect in some way to its surrounding community. But the services that reach the building, once they are inside its four walls, are the responsibility of the owner. What happens to the gas, oil, water, or electricity as it courses through your home is your concern, and nobody else's. If one of the utilities fails to get into your house, the utility company is expected to take care of the matter. If the furnace blows up, or the refrigerator stops running, or the water pipes burst, it's up to you to repair.

The utility companies all spend considerable effort and money maintaining their distribution systems to the many homes they serve. They have work crews laboring day and night, every day of every year, to make certain there is little or no disruption in the service they provide. The networks of pipes and wires that make up the utility-company distribution systems are complex and intricate, and it always seems to the local homeowners that they are forever breaking down. Proportionately speaking, if you consider the millions of miles of electrical cables and pipes those companies must ride herd over, there are very few breakdowns.

The supply systems in any home are far less complicated than what the utility companies must contend with, if only because they are con-

A typical heating system using hot water or steam

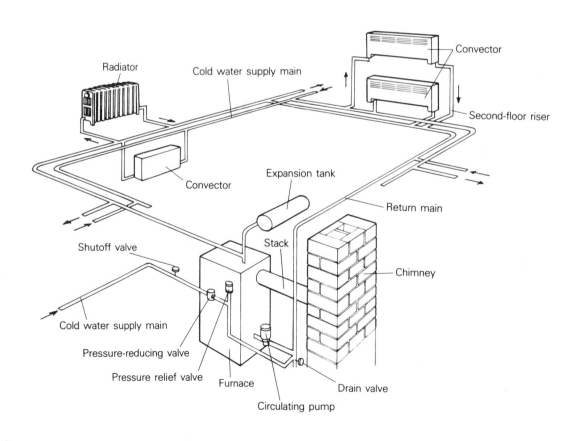

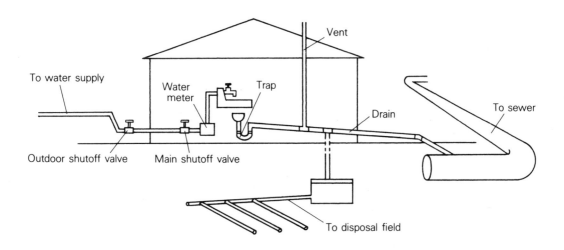

The water supply and sewer systems supporting a residence

siderably smaller. Generally speaking, copper electrical wires and galvanized steel, brass, copper, or plastic plumbing pipes will stand for years before anything happens to them. The trouble is, they can become outdated—not by their specific age, but by the proliferation of appliances and accessories that make increasingly more demands on them. They can also become outdated by a new owner who moves into the building and decides to rearrange the living space in such a way that the plumbing lines no longer go to the proper rooms, or the electrical wiring is not adequate to handle the new demands made on it. All of which is why, when you contemplate any home renovation, you must first consider the state—and location—of the electrical wires, the water supply and drain lines, and the heating pipes or ducts.

PLUMBING

Everybody tends to think of electricity as potentially the most dangerous of the mechanical systems in a house. True, an electrical wire is dangerous enough to kill you. But a broken water supply line is akin to the black plague insofar as a building is concerned. The pressure in the hot and cold water supply pipes is around 60 pounds per square inch (p.s.i.). Open any tap in your house and the water will gush out of it endlessly. Develop a split in one of those pipes inside a wall and thousands of gallons of water a day will pour forth, ruining walls, ceilings, floors, the furnace burner, electrical wiring, and anything else in its path. Get hit with a plumbing disaster that is unabated for a day or two and you might as well sell the house for demolition and move to another neighborhood.

Complicated and massive as it appears, there is really nothing very complex about the plumbing in your home. It is divided into three distinct categories: the hot and cold water supply lines; the drain-waste-vent (DWV) system; and the fixtures (tubs, sinks, toilets).

Water Supply Lines

The water supply begins at the point in your cellar where the 1" cold water main enters the building. As soon as the pipe is inside the basement wall, it is attached to a globe, or gate, valve which, when closed, stops all water from entering the building. This is the **main shutoff valve.** During your inspection of the plumbing system, close the valve to make sure it is functional, then open it again. If it has not been used for years, it may develop a leak at the packing nut directly

under its handle. You can tighten the nut about a quarter-turn with a pipe wrench until the leak stops. If you close the valve and water still comes into the house, the valve is broken and should be replaced, which is a tricky proposition that involves calling your municipal water supply department and asking them to shut off the water at the street valve outside your house. Once that is done, you can remove the main shutoff valve and replace it merely by undoing the coupling nuts on either end of it. One hint about getting the municipality to shut off a street valve: Tell them you have an emergency, and they will react quickly. If you say you merely want to change your main shutoff valve, weeks could pass before anyone shows up, and then it may be at an inconvenient time.

From the main shutoff valve, the cold water line passes through a water meter and then goes directly to the hot water heater, which may constitute your first major renovation. The hot water heater should contain at least 50 gallons of water

The water supply lines in a residence

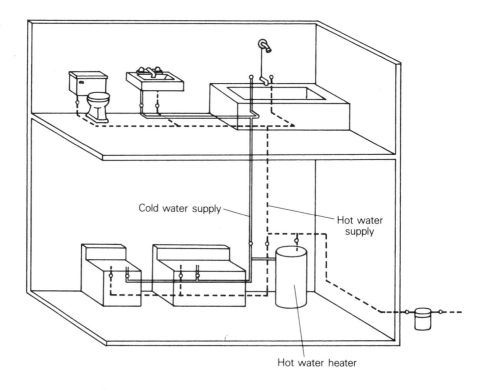

Cold water supply

Hot water supply

Hot water heater

for a family of four, and it can be heated by natural gas, oil, or electricity. Or, the heater may be a set of coils that run through the furnace boiler. If the heater is antiquated, or too small for the number of people in your family, consider changing it. A natural gas–fired hot water heater has a quicker recovery rate than oil-fired or electrically powered units, and natural gas is still the least expensive fossil fuel in most communities; so if there are gas lines entering your building and you have a flock of kids addicted to taking long showers, consider a gas heater as your new unit. Electrically powered heaters are clean and quiet, need no flues to vent fumes outside the building, and are pretty efficient. But they cost quite a bit to operate, the current price of electricity being what it is. Oil-fired heaters can run from your oil furnace and use the same flue the furnace uses. They are efficient, but the added fuel oil you will require during the year makes their operational cost something to look at and compare with other types of units. The heating coils found in the boilers in many old furnaces cause the furance to go on whenever the water is less than its preset temperature (140°F-160°F), whatever the season. Think about how much additional oil that is used during the year. If you find it is too much, the coils can be disconnected anytime, and you can install a separate heater. The one great convenience of heating coils is that you never run out of hot water as long as the furnace is operational, even if you take a 300-gallon shower every morning of the week.

The hot water main begins at the hot water heater and extends throughout the house, usually running parallel to and about 6" away from the cold water main. Both mains should be ¾"- or 1"-diameter copper or galvanized steel pipes. Many old homes were constructed with lead pipes that served one bathroom. Consequently, the mains are something like a half-inch in diameter. Over the years, more bathrooms were added and, depending on when the additions were made, either galvanized steel, brass, or copper piping was connected to the lead lines. If the mains are currently less than ¾" in diameter, you may well

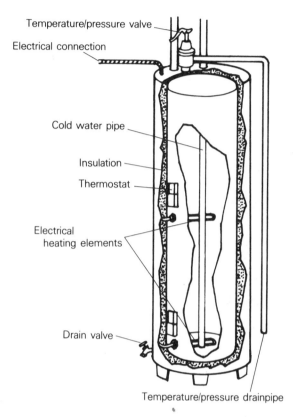

Temperature/pressure valve

Electrical connection

Cold water pipe

Insulation

Thermostat

Electrical heating elements

Drain valve

Temperature/pressure drainpipe

Anatomy of an electric hot water heater

have a problem getting any more than a trickle out of the fourth-floor shower, a trickle that can all but stop if someone turns on the water elsewhere in the house at the same time. If there is a lack of pressure in the bathrooms farthest from the cold water service entrance, consider changing the entire system to ¾"-diameter copper pipes.

The main lines, when they run across the ceiling of the basement or in any other horizontal direction, are called **headers.** The moment they make a right angle and travel vertically up through the walls, they are known as **risers.** As the risers approach each bathroom or the kitchen, smaller-diameter **branch lines** reach out from the mains to each fixture in the house. The branch lines are normally ⅜"-diameter pipes, so that a constant pressure can be maintained in the risers when one of the branches is turned on.

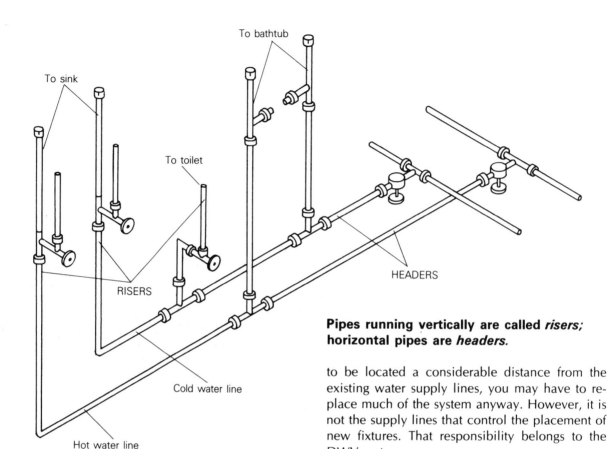

To bathtub

To sink

To toilet

RISERS

HEADERS

Cold water line

Hot water line

Pipes running vertically are called *risers*; horizontal pipes are *headers*.

You can continue to use an existing Rube Goldberg plumbing system if all the pipes go to the right places to satisfy your renovation needs. But the union of different metals causes corrosion at the joints, resulting in a system that is very vulnerable to split pipes and leaking joints. Sooner or later, those joints will give way; and if they happen to be buried in a wall or ceiling somewhere, you are in for an expensive repair job.

If the plumbing system is in any way unsatisfactory, if there are several different kinds of metal used, if there is too little water pressure in the bathrooms or kitchen, or if the whole system is recognizably more than 40 years old, you will save money and avert future disaster by replacing the entire system with copper pipe—even though copper is expensive these days. If you are planning to put in a new kitchen or bathroom that is

to be located a considerable distance from the existing water supply lines, you may have to replace much of the system anyway. However, it is not the supply lines that control the placement of new fixtures. That responsibility belongs to the DWV system.

The Drain-Waste-Vent (DWV) System

Every fixture is connected to the hot and cold water lines, and also to the DWV pipes. While the supply lines are always full of water under a pressure of 40 to 60 p.s.i., the drainpipes are never full of anything except air. The DWV system revolves around two major pipes known as the **house drain** and the **soil stack**. The house drain normally has an inside diameter of 4" and runs horizontally (but at a slight pitch) from the base of the soil stack to the outside of the house, where it connects to the outside sewer line. An older home may have its house drain buried under the cellar floor, but often the drain will be visible as it runs along one wall of the basement.

The soil stack is always a 4"-diameter vertical pipe that extends from one end of the house drain all the way through the roof. Every drain from every fixture in the house connects to the soil stack at some point, usually with a 2", 1½", or 1¼" drainpipe.

Any old house that has its original soil stack and house drain has 4" cast iron piping. Cast iron is heavy and must be held together with oakum and melted lead, which is stuffed into an enlarged end of each pipe section, and around the base of the smaller "straight" end of the joining section. Cast iron will last for about 40 years, but when it begins to weaken, you can literally stick your fist through it.

Cast iron is so heavy that it is rarely manufactured in lengths of more than 5 feet. Still it is awkward to assemble, since you must have a lead melting stove and some other special tools, and installation requires at least two men. Modern versions of the cast iron bell-and-spigot pipe are called hubless pipe. Hubless pipe can be assembled with a neoprene grommet and clamps, but it, too, is heavy and awkward to work with. The installation of a cast iron house drain and

stack is no job for amateurs, and to hire someone to install them can cost well over $3,000.

Polyvinyl chloride (PVC) plastic pipe has recently come to the rescue. PVC drainpipe is manufactured in both 3" and 4" diameters; it is light and easily assembled; and in most cities in the United States it is now acceptable by the building codes. Not enough time has passed since the invention of plastic pipe to verify its manufacturers' claims that it will outlast cast iron, but even if it doesn't, it is infinitely cheaper (about a dollar a running foot), lighter, and easier to work with. If you need to replace your soil stack and/or house drain, and your local building code permits the use of PVC or ABS (acrylonitrile-butadiene-styrene) plastic drainpipe, the hardest part of the job will be to disassemble the old cast iron soil stack and house drain and get rid of them. From then on, this once expensive, time-consuming renovation can easily be done by any homeowner—provided he or she understands the principles behind making the drain line and vent connections, which are as follows:

Sometimes a second stack must be added to the DWV system.

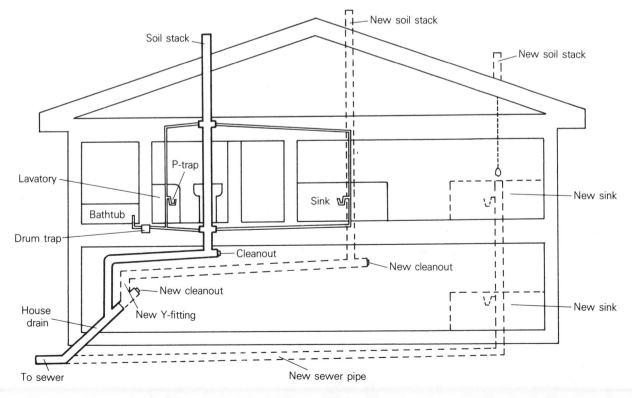

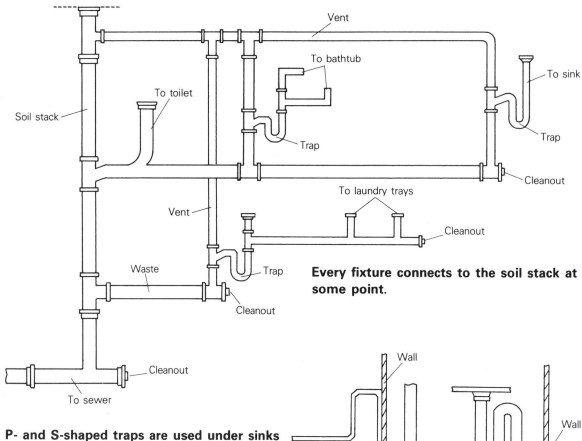

Every fixture connects to the soil stack at some point.

P- and S-shaped traps are used under sinks and modern bathtub installations. Drum traps are buried in the floor near bathtubs but are no longer considered sanitary.

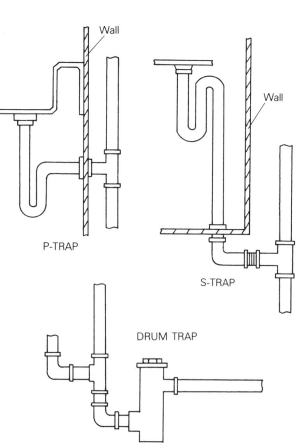

Every fixture *must be* connected to the soil stack, which carries all wastes to the house drain and then out of the house to the sewer. The fixtures are attached to the stack by branch drain lines that vary from 1¼″ to 2″ in diameter. But there is a danger of waste materials lodging in the system and decomposing, which will cause gases, odors, and waste to back up into the fixtures. It is also possible for insects and other vermin to enter a house by crawling through the drainpipes and emerging from the fixtures. To prevent all of this from happening, two things are done when the DWV is installed in a house: vent pipes are attached to every fixture, and each individual drain line has a water trap built into it.

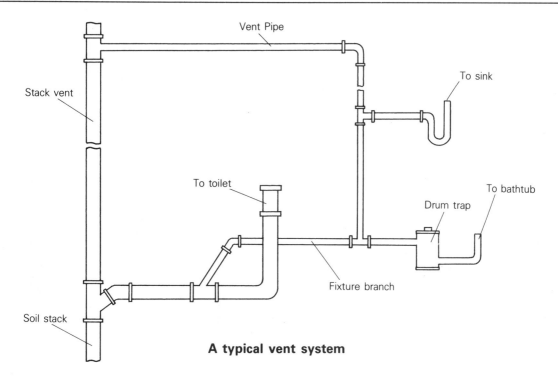

A typical vent system

Traps. These are those P- or S-shaped pieces of pipe connected directly under the drain outlet of every bathtub, sink, and shower in the building. Toilets, by nature of their design, always have water in their bowls, which acts as a trap in itself. All traps hold a certain amount of water in the bottom of their curves, which prevents any gases or vermin from passing through them to the house. It should be noted that all traps are either removable (by loosening the coupling nuts at each end of their curve) or have a threaded plug (cleanout) at the bottom of their lowest curve, so they can be entered for cleaning purposes. Since there is always water in the traps, never open one unless you have first placed a pan under it, or the floor (and you) will get wet.

Vents. The vent pipes connected to each fixture travel through the walls and then connect to the soil stack at a point above the highest fixture in the building. They enter the stack at an upward angle, so that only air can get into them. The air comes from the top of the soil stack, which ex-

The water supply hookup with sinks or tubs

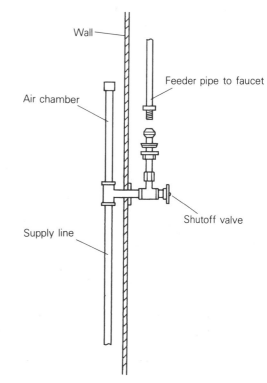

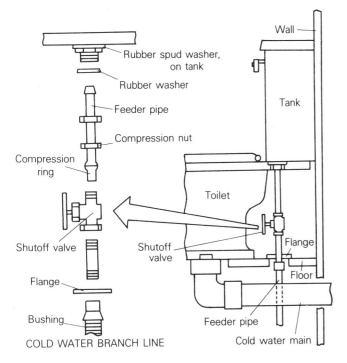

Rubber spud washer, on tank

Rubber washer

Feeder pipe

Compression nut

Compression ring

Shutoff valve

Flange

Bushing

COLD WATER BRANCH LINE

Wall

Tank

Toilet

Shutoff valve

Flange

Floor

Feeder pipe

Cold water main

A typical cold water supply hookup with a toilet

which require only a connection to the cold water main. The cold water branch line comes out of the wall or floor under the left side of the toilet tank (as you face the wall) from a shutoff valve. A ⅜" feeder line leads directly to the underside of the toilet tank, where it is connected to the tank flush valve.

The only visible part of the DWV system is the drain branch line from the soil stack, which you can see as it comes out of the walls. The fixture trap is connected between the branch line and the drain tailpipe of the sink. Otherwise, most of the soil stack and drain lines, as well as all of the vent pipes, are hidden in the walls of the house. Usually (but not always), the walls that contain plumbing pipes are interior walls, which need to be no thicker than the normal 5" or 6" unless they are hiding the stack.

The stack will never have less than a 3" inside diameter. But the outside diameter of a 4" cast

tends through the roof and is left open to the atmosphere. If a fixture is too far away from the stack to be conveniently vented to it, its vent pipe can be run straight up through the roof, so that the fixture will be properly vented to the outside.

Where the Pipes Are Hiding. You can usually see the water supply lines and house drain, as well as the base of the soil stack, in the cellar. The supply lines are attached to the underside of the first-floor joists until they reach the base of a wall and turn upward to rise through the house. The pipes are next visible when they emerge from the bathroom or kitchen walls directly beneath a sink or behind a shower stall or tub, where they immediately end at a valve. A ⅜" feeder pipe extends from the valve to the tailpipe of each faucet. The hot and cold water lines almost always travel parallel to each other; thus, the feeder lines are also parallel, with the hot water pipe to the left (as you face the wall the pipes emerge from). The only exception is toilets,

Anatomy of a fixture hookup, including the trap arrangement

Sink overflow

Flexible copper tube

Flange

Rubber washer

Stopper valve

Tailpiece

Rubber washer

To water supply

Angle stop valve

Rubber washer

Drainpipe

Slip couplings

Trap

Soil stack

Wall

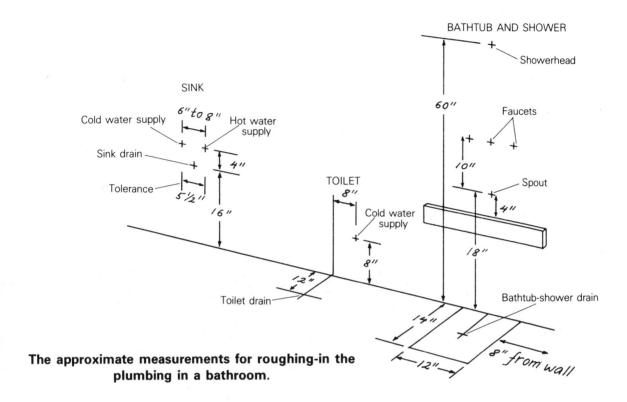

The approximate measurements for roughing-in the plumbing in a bathroom.

iron pipe may be as much as 5", which means that the wall that houses it will have to be one or two inches thicker than normal. It is not uncommon in old houses to carry the stack up through a series of closets, where the stack can then be boxed off and pretty much kept out of everybody's way. In urban row houses, the closet line is very often somewhere in the middle of the building.

Fixtures

The important point to remember about the tubs, sinks, lavatories (bathroom sinks), basins, toilets, and shower stalls that you plan to remove or install during your renovation is to bring the water supply lines and drainpipes to their exact location. You do not need to install a new bathtub, for example, as soon as its pipe connections emerge from the wall. You can cap the pipes and not put the tub in place or install the pipelines for

years, if you wish. But it is considerably cheaper and easier to do the roughing-in work when you are renovating the entire plumbing system, rather than break open a wall or two at some later time and have to make connections in pipes that are already tightly fitted between the wall studs.

Not only must the fixtures be accounted for, but also the supply lines and drains for dishwashers, clothes washers, ice cube–making refrigerators, and work basins in the cellar or a projected laundry room. Since the installation of any fixture does not require that the walls or floors be opened (if the pipes already emerge from them), all you need to do during your planning stage is determine *exactly* where you want each fixture to be. What the fixture will be, and which manufacturer you will buy it from, come under the heading of decoration; but you do have to make a selection before you do your roughing-in, so that you have exact measurements to work with when determining where your pipes will emerge from the walls.

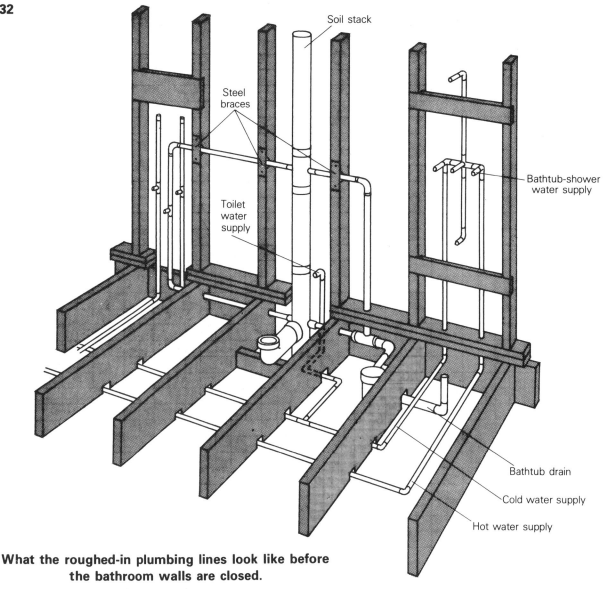

Soil stack

Steel braces

Toilet water supply

Bathtub-shower water supply

Bathtub drain

Cold water supply

Hot water supply

What the roughed-in plumbing lines look like before the bathroom walls are closed.

PLANNING PLUMBING

If you can avoid the expense of adding a new soil stack, you will usually save a considerable amount of money and labor. On the other hand, if using the existing stack requires you to knock down too many walls or build too many partitions just to satisfy the plumbing system as it now stands, you may end up spending more money, time, and effort than you would if you put in a new stack. So before any work begins, you have to do some balancing between what you want, what you can afford, and what you have to work with. Be careful to take into account every possible fixture and appliance that will need water, and make sure that the plumbing system is designed to support them all, wherever they are to be situated in the building.

In general, there are two ways of making full use of a single soil stack and house drain: **stacked plumbing** and **back-to-back plumbing.**

Stacked Plumbing. Most multileveled houses rely on stacked plumbing. Since one soil stack can handle the waste from innumerable fixtures, it is common to place bathrooms more or less above each other so that all of their fixtures can connect to the same stack. The inhibiting factor here is the position of the stack: if it runs up the outside corner of the building, all of the fixtures in every room wind up being pretty much aligned one on top of the other. But building codes have certain requirements concerning the distance between the soil stack and fixtures—toilets, for example, are not allowed to be more than 15″ away from the stack that services them. So if the stack is in the same corner of every bathroom in the house, all of the bathrooms will probably look very much alike.

If the stack is in a partition wall, however, you have considerably more leeway. The bathrooms can be staggered from one side of the wall to the other, and while the toilets will always be against that wall, there can be any number of variations in where the other fixtures are installed.

Back-to-Back Plumbing. Back-to-back plumbing is another money- and space-saving device. In this kind of arrangement, a stack can not only handle infinite numbers of fixtures, but it allows those fixtures to connect to it at approximately the same point. Thus, you can have two bathrooms next to each other, with a partition wall between them. If the stack runs up the middle of that partition wall, you can have toilets connecting to both sides of it. Again, the bathrooms may look identical by the time you are finished arranging all of the fixtures in them, but at least you will have had to install only one stack.

WHO DOES THE PLUMBING?

Some large municipalities insist that all major plumbing in any residence be done by professionals. In the majority of communities, the homeowner can do most or all of the plumbing work himself, so long as the finished work meets with the standards of the local plumbing code. In

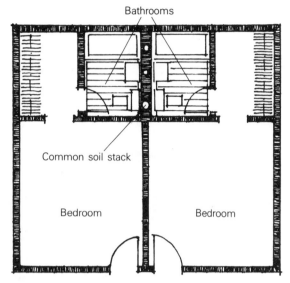

Bathrooms with side-by-side plumbing can use the same soil stack, but the rooms are liable to look somewhat alike.

terms of cost, the more plumbing you can do on your own, the less expensive it will be. If you must replace or install a new stack and you can use plastic pipe, don't hesitate to take on the job. If you need to upgrade old water supply lines or add new ones, you can use plastic pipe in many areas, but more likely the local codes will demand galvanized steel or copper. Copper pipe and tubing is expensive, so all the more reason you should consider doing the work yourself. Working with copper, once you get the hang of making neat, watertight sweat-solder joints, is almost as easy as working with plastic. It will take you about four sweat joints to learn how to solder.

When you assemble your plumbing system, there are only four working guidelines to follow:

1. Have as few pipes as possible.

2. Be sure all your joints are watertight.

3. Keep your pipe runs as short as you can.

4. Make as few bends in your pipe runs as you can.

Beyond these rules, there are numerous precautions and demands listed in your local plumbing code that must be met for the sake of your safety and health.

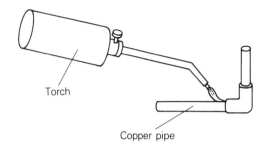

Torch

Copper pipe

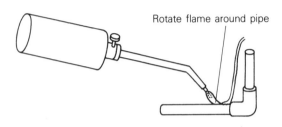

Rotate flame around pipe

Sweat-soldering copper pipe is not difficult, but it does take a little practice to learn.

GAS LINES

Gas pipes are always made out of black iron, and you can identify them in your basement by their color. The diameter of a gas pipe will vary according to what and how many appliances it serves, and how far the gas main must travel through the house. Today, natural gas is used primarily for cooking, drying clothes, firing furnaces, and running hot water heaters. The service line is brought through the basement wall to a meter that is owned by the gas utility company. The meter connects to the black iron pipe system inside the house, and from that point on all of the connections to the oven, cooktop, furnace, heater, or clothes dryer are made by a plumber. Aside

from being highly flammable, gas is also explosive and the pipe connections require specially sealed joints to prevent any gas from leaking into the air. Although the work is not any more difficult than making joints in plumbing lines, you should hire a qualified plumber to make any gas connections in your house. Whatever he costs you, the job will be done correctly and you will have the peace of mind of knowing that the potential bomb you are living with has been defused.

Older houses, particularly the Victorian structures in many large cities, used gas as a source of light. Consequently, many old urban houses have gas pipes lurking in all kinds of walls. The pipes were probably disconnected long ago, but they may be still there. Once in a while, their capped ends may even jut out of a wall or ceiling. Victorian homeowners also used gas logs in their hearths, so you may find some pipes and shutoff valves in or around your fireplace.

An old, disconnected gas-pipe line can often be reused merely by uncapping it and connecting it to an appliance and the gas main; modern-day renovators have been known to install gas-burning chandeliers and fireplace logs. The logs provide a colorful, flickering flame but not much heat, so don't expect them to replace your furnace next winter.

If you mean to incorporate natural gas as a source of energy in your renovation, plan for it early; also, check with your local gas company to be sure the utility is willing and able to service your house. Gas companies in many locales will provide a free inspection of the gas lines in a residence, and tell you exactly what you can and cannot do with the existing pipes. For example, if you have a half-inch main in your house, but want to use the gas to operate a barbeque 50 feet beyond the back door, you may be told that moving the gas from the service entrance at the front of your basement, through the house, and out to the backyard requires a larger main. At that point, you have to decide whether the installation cost of new piping, and the barbeque, is worth the expense.

Alternatively, if you move into an old house and decide not to use its gas lines, you can disconnect them and thread caps over the ends of the pipes. Also, remember to call the gas company and have them take away their meter or you will be billed the monthly minimum for a service you aren't using.

ELECTRICITY

Electricity can cause fires, and building codes are designed to protect people from such hazards. When it comes to electricity, building codes can be extremely strict about the standards that must be met. Some cities won't let anyone touch an electrical system unless he is a licensed electrician. Most communities permit a homeowner to do all of his own electrical work up to, but not including, hooking up the distribution panel (fuse box).

Most of the homes built in America before 1960 are now underpowered. Their electrical systems simply do not provide enough amperage to meet the needs of all the appliances used in an average household. Moreover, the power companies that service most of the houses in America, while they are constantly upgrading and expanding their own facilities, are not yet equipped to upgrade the incoming service to all of their customers.

The chances are very great that if you have just moved into an old house and you want to renovate it, you will find it is woefully underelectrified: there are not nearly enough outlets along every wall (most building codes prescribe one every 6 to 10 feet); there is only one branch line serving the kitchen; there are precious few overhead lights; and there may be no way of plugging in even a small one-room air conditioner without blowing fuses. Upgrading any electrical system begins by first asking your local electric company if it can supply you with more power. If the answer is yes, you can go ahead and hire an electrician to add more branch lines and install a circuit breaker board. Or you can start pulling your own wires through the walls and installing the outlets and switches wherever you want them. But if you decide to do the work yourself, *make very certain that you adhere to local electrical standards as well as the National Electrical Code.* If your renovation is a major one and you have had to get a

A typical electrical system

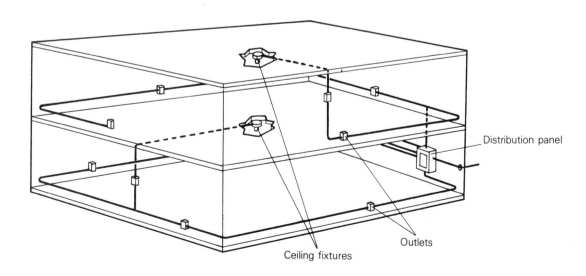

Distribution panel

Outlets

Ceiling fixtures

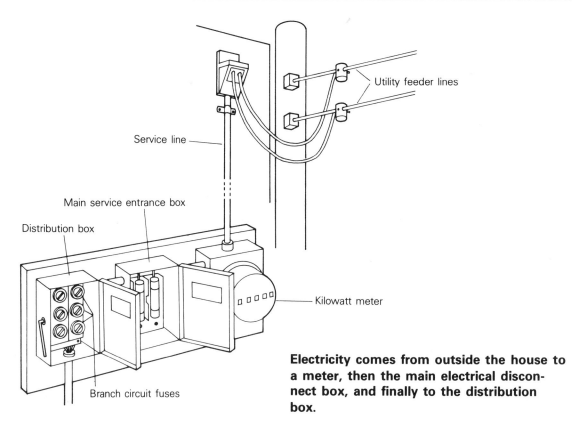

Service line

Main service entrance box

Distribution box

Utility feeder lines

Kilowatt meter

Branch circuit fuses

Electricity comes from outside the house to a meter, then the main electrical disconnect box, and finally to the distribution box.

building permit, municipal inspectors will have specified stages during the work process at which they will check what you have done.

HOW MUCH JUICE?

How much electricity enters any house depends on the size of the service line that enters it. The service line is just a fat cable containing three or more copper wires that are connected first to a meter, and then terminate at a service entrance box. The main box has a handle on its outside which must be pulled before you can open the box, which contains the main circuit breaker(s). By pulling the handle to open the door of the box, you automatically shut off all of the electricity coming into the building.

The main service box is screwed to a board that is fixed to your basement wall. Right next to it is the distribution box containing clusters of fuses and/or circuit breakers. Each fuse or circuit

breaker controls one of the branch circuits that carry electricity to different parts of the house. The fuses and circuit breakers are always labeled according to the amount of amperage they will permit to flow through the branch line without disengaging and shutting off the electricity. Thus, a 15-ampere fuse controlling the branch line to your kitchen will placidly do nothing as long as your refrigerator is humming along drawing its 10 amperes of power every time its motor starts up. But as soon as you plug in a toaster on the same line and it draws the 7 amperes it needs to operate, the branch circuit is drawing more electricity than its wires can carry without heating up to the point of combustion. So the fuse or circuit breaker "blows" and, in doing so, it breaks the connection between the electricity coming from the service line to the branch line.

Modern households require at least 100 amperes of electricity. Given the power demands of air conditioners, color television sets, refrigerator/freezers, hot water heaters, ranges, and all those smaller appliances, 150 amperes is more reasonable. And if you mean to heat your house with electricity or use central air conditioning, 200 amperes is barely enough to meet your needs.

Most electrical companies provide some sort of electrical survey free of charge, and this can help you determine whether the existing wiring is adequate to meet your electrical needs. The utility report will also determine what size service cable is required, suggest the number of circuits needed inside the house, and list the wire sizes to be used in each circuit. Actually, most branch circuits use #12-gauge copper wire these days. It is more than likely that the original wiring in an old house was installed with the much larger #10 wire, which means it can handle added amperage very easily—even if the wires are 40 years old (copper wire deteriorates very slowly).

Certain large-power appliances, such as air conditioners, electric ranges, and electric hot water heaters, must be given their own branch circuits, which are generally fused at 30 or more amperes ("amps"). These particular circuits can be installed as a matter of course, along with any new branch lines.

In the majority of old houses, you can still employ the existing system and merely supplement it with more branch lines that derive their power from increased amperage brought into the house. But there can be some special problems with new wiring, particularly if part of the house is to be renovated into apartments. Every apartment will normally have its own meter, and therefore its own fuse box and own branch lines. The distribution box can be in the cellar near the main circuit breaker, or it can be installed upstairs in each apartment, which is by far more convenient for the apartment dweller. But if the house has not previously been divided into apartments, its present wiring winds all over the building. You may have branch circuits that include parts of more than one apartment, in which case it is a difficult, time-consuming, and therefore expensive task to separate the wiring. In fact, it is so

A secondary distribution box can be connected to the main box and placed anywhere in the house.

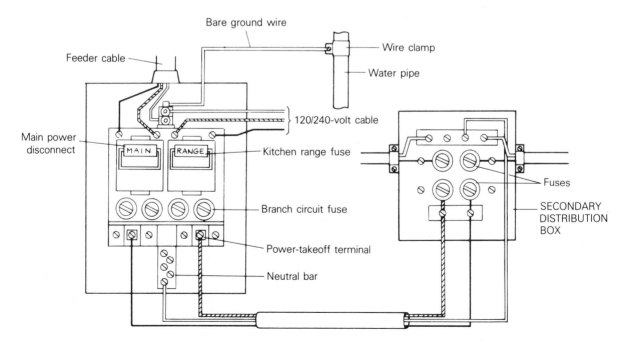

Bare ground wire

Feeder cable

Wire clamp

Water pipe

120/240-volt cable

Main power disconnect

MAIN   RANGE

Kitchen range fuse

Branch circuit fuse

Power-takeoff terminal

Neutral bar

Fuses

SECONDARY DISTRIBUTION BOX

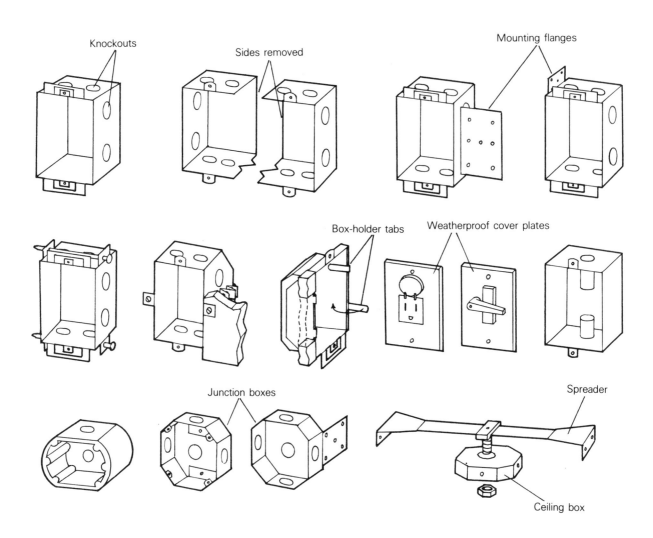

Knockouts

Sides removed

Mounting flanges

Box-holder tabs

Weatherproof cover plates

Junction boxes

Spreader

Ceiling box

Electrical boxes are designed to meet any need.

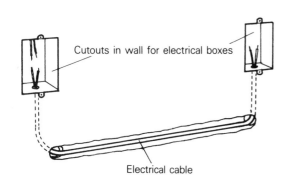

Cutouts in wall for electrical boxes

Electrical cable

Cables must be run from box to box before you put the switches fixtures and outlets in them.

time consuming that many professional electricians often refuse to do it; it is so expensive that you may find it cheaper to disconnect some of the old wires and simply run new ones.

Electrical work involves determining where you want to add outlets, overhead fixtures, and switches. Number 12 cable must be run from electrical box to electrical box and then as far as the distribution box. Each of the electrical boxes is a small metal rectangle, octagon, or square which has cutouts stamped in it to permit pieces of cable to enter and leave it. A hole is cut in the walls for each box and then the cable is run through the walls, ceiling, and floors to the next box. When all of the boxes have been nailed or screwed to framing members inside the walls and the cables are inserted in them, either a switch or an outlet is connected to the bared ends of the wires coming from the cables. The branch line is then connected to the terminals attached to a receptacle in the distribution box designed to accept either a circuit breaker or a fuse.

It is a simple matter to run electrical cable to exactly the right places in any unfinished wall—that is, a wall that has been framed, but is not covered with either plaster or wallboard. An electrician can run wires through a moderately sized house in a couple of days if the walls are all no more than framing members. But snaking wires through a 100-year-old plaster-and-lath wall is, comparatively speaking, a nightmare: holes must be knocked in the plaster for the electrical boxes, stiff cable has to be pushed up or down the walls between unseen studs and fire breaks. More holes must be drilled through the sole plates of the walls, the flooring and the top plates of the wall beneath, or worked gingerly between the joists of a ceiling. It can take days to install a couple of branch lines in an old (or even a new) building that has finished walls, floors, and ceilings. So if you intend to knock down some walls and build partitions, the time to do the electrical work is after the studs are in place and before they have been covered.

Electricians commonly estimate the cost of a job in terms of so much for each electrical box

they install. The price, which varies from $15 to $35 per box, takes into account the amount of cable needed and the length of time the entire job will cost. Just remember that at, say, $30 a box (whether it contains a lighting fixture, switch, or outlet does not matter), you can run your rewiring bill up very quickly. Normally added to the per-box cost is a separate fee for installing a new distribution panel: this can be upward of $250, depending on the size of the panel and the number of circuit interrupters to be put in.

Pulling wires through walls and ceilings that are closed is a time-consuming chore. Have an electrician do it.

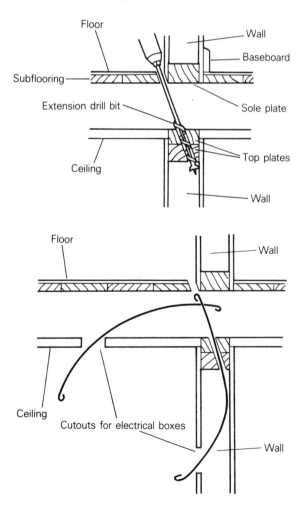

PLANNING FOR OUTLETS

There are three types of outlets to be considered when you plan a renovation of your house wiring. **Convenience** outlets are the double-socket types used for lamps, small appliances, and so forth. **Utility** outlets are specially designed for kitchens and workshops, and are serviced by a 20-amp branch circuit. They are installed anywhere you intend to use appliances that draw large quantities of power. **Heavy-duty** outlets are designed for special equipment such as air conditioners, ranges, and clothes dryers. The heavy-duty outlet is designed specifically to accept the plug attached to the one unit that will be used on the branch circuit.

When planning a revamped (or new) electrical system there are several items to bear in mind:

1. Outlets should be between 6 and 10 feet apart along every wall of every room, and about 12" above the top of the baseboard. If there is an overhead fixture in the room, keep it on a branch circuit separate from the outlets so that you will always have some source of power in the room.

2. In a kitchen, install one outlet for every appliance you own, then add one more outlet for future needs. Refrigerators and toasters draw tremendous amounts of power when they're first turned on, so they should be plugged into separate branch lines. Actually, two or three branch lines serving a kitchen is not outlandish. At least one branch should be fused at 20 amps to handle your small appliances.

3. Be sure there is at least one outlet in every bathroom.

4. When there is to be a workshop in the basement, provide ample outlets for the machinery to be used. If some of your tools are stationary power units, they will require a 20-amp branch line; half-horsepower saw motors, for instance, draw a lot of current while they are getting up to their running speeds.

5. There should be outlets at both the top and the bottom of every flight of stairs, for vacuum cleaning.

6. Even if you don't plan to have them right away, provide wiring for dishwashers, clothes washers, and dryers. If nothing else, the presence of ample wiring enhances the resale value of the house.

7. All exterior outlets must be weatherproofed according to the local building code. (In some locales it is not necessary to use conduit, the traditional protective device for electrical wiring.)

8. Wherever you install a stove, remember that its timer, light, and clock operate on a separate branch line than the one that supplies the cooking cavity. Gas stoves and ranges also need a separate outlet.

9. You can buy specially designed childproof outlets that prevent small children from hurting themselves. If your children are small, at least put the special units in their bedrooms.

10. Large window air conditioners must have special outlets and their own branch circuits. In some communities the building code insists that you provide outlets for an air conditioner in every room.

Exterior electrical outlets must be weatherproofed.

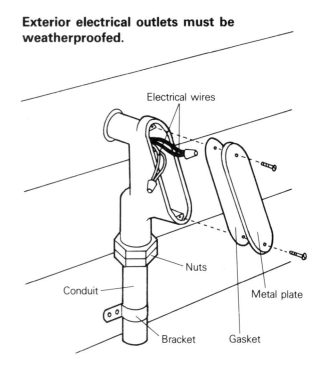

LIGHTING FIXTURES

Insofar as bringing the cables to a fixture position is concerned, the labor involved is no different than that for installing an outlet. The fixture can be mounted in the wall or a ceiling, or it can be recessed between the joists or studs. If the unit is mounted flush against the wall or ceiling, only the electrical box need be in the wall or ceiling itself. But if the entire fixture is to be recessed, it must be given a wooden frame to hold it in place, so some carpentry work has to be done before the light is installed.

Recessed fixtures are sexy, but it takes more of them to adequately light a room that you would need if they were flush-mounted to the ceiling. Also, before you decide to put recessed fixtures in a 12-foot ceiling, first consider the inconvenience of getting out a high step ladder every time you need to replace a light bulb. Recessed lights are, however, ideal for low ceilings, where a surface-mounted unit would tend to make the ceiling seem even lower.

As you select your lighting fixtures and plan their location, bear in mind that you can have not only standard incandescent bulbs and fluorescents, but high-intensity lamps as well. High-intensity lamps last almost as long as fluorescents; both use less electricity than incandescents. Fluorescents can be extremely effective when hidden under the bottom of kitchen cabinets over the work counter, or behind the crown molding in a high ceiling; in workshops; and hung above a glass or partially glass ceiling. But you have to know exactly where they will be placed at the time the wiring work is being done. When you are planning your lighting also take into account the following:

1. If you want the hanging lamp in your dining room to be exactly over the center of the table, make sure you know where the table is going to stand before you put the light up.

2. Electrical boxes are not anchored between the joists of a ceiling in such a way that they can support an inordinately heavy ceiling fixture. If the fixture is a heavy one, best you install a load-

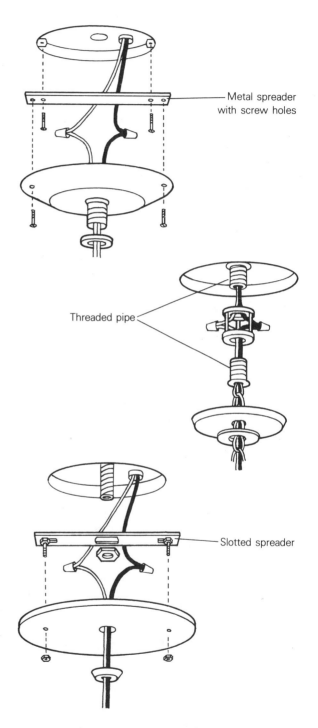

Metal spreader with screw holes

Threaded pipe

Slotted spreader

Some of the ways overhead fixtures are held in place

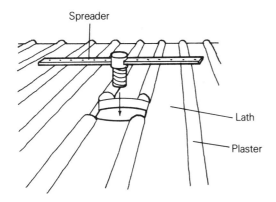

If a fixture is unusually heavy, add a load-bearing spreader between the joists to support it. If the ceiling is plaster and lath, use a short spreader that rests on the lath.

bearing spreader between the joists or a piece of pipe that can carry most of the weight of the unit.

3. Allow for lights in the attic, cellar, and closets.

4. Exterior lights on the front and rear of the building are a good idea for safety as well as a deterrent to housebreakers. They should meet all standards of the local building code and should light all doorways. That means if you have an entrance under a stoop as well as at the top of it, you will need two lights.

5. Electricians hate to drill holes through masonry and they are liable to charge you extra for it, but there should be no exposed wiring running up the front or back of your building to the outdoor lights. If the wires are encased in a conduit, the pipes don't look much better. So even if you must pay extra for it, have the wires hidden behind the outside walls.

6. If you want the use of a gas lamp outside your building and the law permits it, make provisions for it from the beginning. In some places the gas company will install the lamp for you (for a fee) at the same time they are bringing service into the house.

Exterior lights can be controlled by a photoelectric cell that automatically turns them on when the sun goes down, and off again at dawn.

Switches

Once you have determined where your lights will be placed, give some hard thought to the location of their switches:

1. Don't put the bathroom light switch *behind* the hinged side of the door. It should be on the latch side, so the lights can be turned on without having to enter the room, close the door behind you, and then fumble in the dark as you feel around for the switch.

2. Place switches so they are low enough for your children to reach.

3. Put all of the switches in the house at exactly the same height and, whenever possible, in the same position just inside the latch side of the doors.

4. One switch can control more than one fixture. But if you have three or four lights in a kitchen ceiling, for instance, you'll want to control each of them with its own switch so that you can use only as much light in the room as is needed at one time.

The wire hookup for a pair of three-way switches controlling a stairway or hall light, plus a convenience outlet somewhere

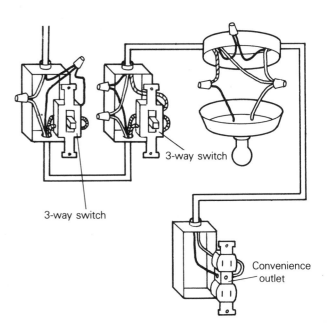

3-way switch

3-way switch

Convenience outlet

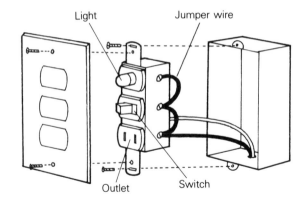

How a combination switch-light-outlet is wired

5. Install three-way switches at the top and bottom of stairways or at the ends of long halls. It is extremely inconvenient to have to run down two flights of stairs to shut off the hall light and then pick your way back up to bed in the dark.

6. Dimmer switches cost a little more than regular switches, but they are excellent for controlling the amount of light you use and will increase the longevity of your bulbs.

7. Combination switch-outlets are a thrifty way of getting an extra outlet into a guest bedroom or a bathroom without paying for the installation of another electrical box.

8. Closet lights can be controlled by switches or pull chains. You can also buy a light with a large button at its base, specially designed to operate automatically: the light is placed near the closet door so that it turns on when the door is opened, and off when the door closes.

REWIRING CHECKLIST

When you plan the rewiring of your house, bear these items in mind:

1. Add more service to your house, preferably 100 or 150 amps.

2. Install new meters in each apartment.

3. Install circuit breakers instead of fuses. It is easier to turn on a circuit breaker than it is to change a fuse, which you may not have handy when the old fuses blow.

4. Put a circuit breaker box inside each apartment.

5. Plan enough conveniently located outlets, fixtures, and switches to meet all of your needs in the future as well as at present.

6. Install separate branch lines with the proper wiring, fused to the correct amperage, for electric ranges, hot water heaters, clothes dryers, and air conditioning units.

7. Allow the proper wiring for both air conditioner and furnace thermostats.

8. Allow for wiring all intercom and door-buzzer systems.

How the wires for various doorbell systems are hooked up

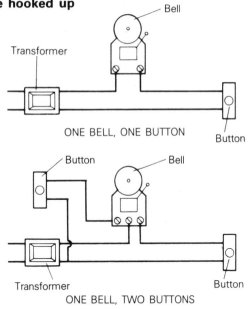

ONE BELL, ONE BUTTON

ONE BELL, TWO BUTTONS

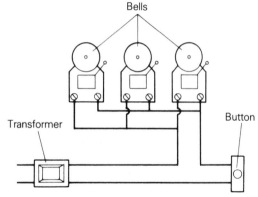

THREE BELLS IN DIFFERENT LOCATIONS, ONE BUTTON

HEATING

The furnaces and heating systems in old houses can be deceptive. They may look and even sound antiquated and appear in need of replacement. But a careful check of the system may also reveal that it is more than adequate, or that by replacing the burner or a pump, the furnace can go right on producing heat throughout your building. If that is the case, don't be too quick about replacing the entire system. Heating systems are expensive to buy and even more costly to install.

Old homes may have one of three types of heating systems: a hot water or steam system, both of which require pipes leading up from the furnace to each radiator in the house; or, one that uses forced warm air, which is pushed through ducts that end at grills in each room. The forced-air systems are what most contractors install in new construction, but older houses usually have a steam or hot water system.

The problems with steam and hot water systems are the noise they make and the unsightly radiators all over the house. The noise is not a function of the fact that the system has been in operation for 30 or 40 years; it is caused by the water in it being heated and then cooled, and being forced up pipes and then rolling back down. There is not much you can do about the hissing, rattling, radiator clanks, and gurgles. You can replace unsightly radiators with modern baseboard units that are about 12″ high, 4″ thick, and as long as you want them to be (they are sold in 2- and 4-foot sections).

Presuming that you elect to save your money and spend it on other renovations, you may still have the problem of getting a radiator into any new room you have constructed. It is possible to extend a heating system the same way a plumbing system can be extended—by adding more pipes that end at more radiators. However, heating systems are carefully designed (even if they are old) and balanced to allow them to operate

with equal efficiency in all parts of the house. You could throw that balance off by haphazardly adding two or three radiators here and there around the house. So even if you plan to install the new radiators yourself, have their locations evaluated by a professional heating engineer before you do any work.

If the rooms you want to heat cannot be sustained by your existing system, you have a couple of options. You might install a space-heating system for the new space. Conceivably, if you have natural gas service for your cooking and clothes drying, the space heater, which could be recessed in a wall, might be gas-fired. Or you could consider electric baseboard heaters. Electricity provides a clean, maintenance-free heating system that can be installed just about anywhere. But in most parts of the country, it will cost an arm and a leg to operate.

If you must replace the furnace, or the boiler, or both, you are in for $2,000 to $3,000 in expenses, no matter what fuel the unit uses. However, some old furnaces can be converted from one fuel to another at considerably less expense, and there are now a number of heat-saving devices that can be added to different types of furnaces to help you get a little more efficiency out of an existing system.

Exactly what you need to do with the particular system you have can only be decided when you have specific information in hand. To get that information, call in an expert and buy a report from him. In many communities, the gas company will provide a free inspection and evaluation, not only for an existing gas furnace, but for making the conversion from oil to gas. One of the things you ought to find out from whatever experts you talk to is what the price of gas, compared to oil, will be in the near future. There is no longer a federal ceiling on the price of natural gas. It will very likely be just as expensive as oil in the near future, if it is not already there.

No matter what you decide to do about your heating system, decide to do it before you take on any renovation in the house. It may turn out, for example, that you need to run some more

FREE-STANDING RADIATORS

SUSPENDED RADIATORS

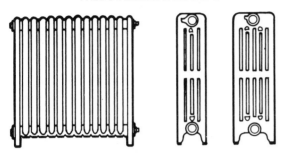

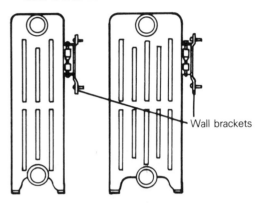

— Wall brackets

Typical hot water or steam radiators

NONFERROUS BASEBOARD RADIATOR

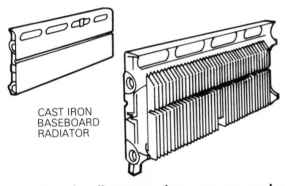

CAST IRON
BASEBOARD
RADIATOR

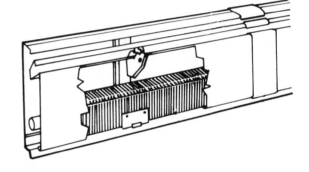

**Baseboard radiators are low, narrow, and can be as long as
you wish. The cast iron variety can be used with either
steam or hot water systems, while nonferrous radiators can
be used with hot water systems only.**

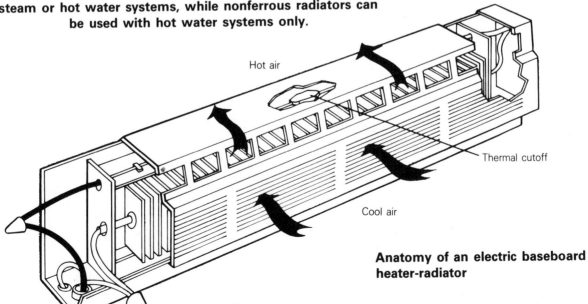

Hot air

Thermal cutoff

Cool air

**Anatomy of an electric baseboard
heater-radiator**

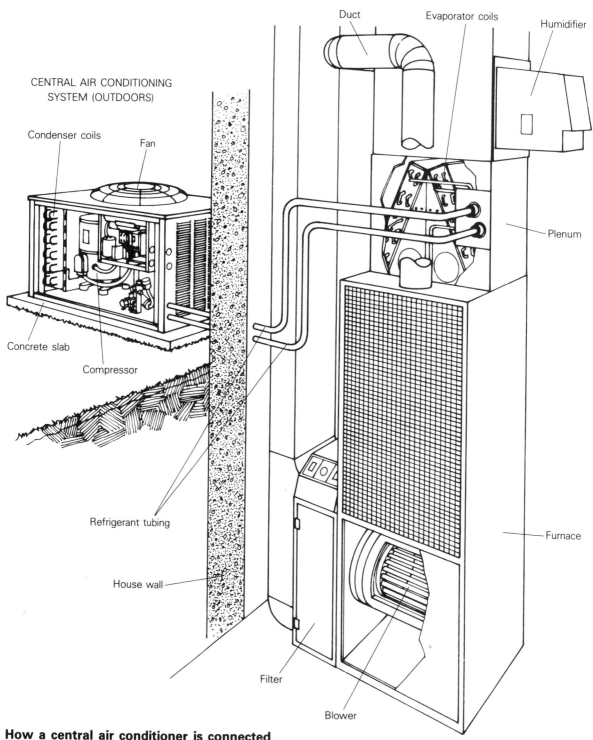

CENTRAL AIR CONDITIONING
SYSTEM (OUTDOORS)

Condenser coils

Fan

Duct

Evaporator coils

Humidifier

Plenum

Concrete slab

Compressor

Refrigerant tubing

House wall

Furnace

Filter

Blower

**How a central air conditioner is connected
to a forced-air duct system**

FORCED-AIR DUCT SYSTEM (INDOORS)

pipes or ducts through the house, and these will have to be hidden in the walls. Obviously, it is less expensive and infinitely easier to . do that when some or all of the walls have already been opened or are not yet closed.

AIR CONDITIONING

Some communities require that electrical service for air conditioners and outlets be provided for every room of the house. The air conditioning of a home can be done with room window units or via a central air conditioning system. In either case, the cost of running the machinery is very expensive, since all air conditioners must draw a considerable amount of electrical power. Central air conditioning systems include a large unit that is placed outdoors near a side of the house, and which sends its cooled air through ducts. In most cases, if you have a forced-air heating system, the ducts already in the building can be used to service an air conditioning system. If you don't have a forced-air heating system, the duct system can be provided by installing plastic pipes in the walls, or by using the conventional rectangular sheet metal–type ducts. In either case, some of the walls will have to be opened up to one degree or another. Obviously, pipes are easier and less complicated to install than the larger metal ducts. The air conditioner itself costs in the neighborhood of $1,000, and then there is the installation fee. Installation involves placing the unit outside on a concrete or other very stable foundation. It must then be connected by ducts to the house duct system.

While installing a central air conditioning system is expensive, compare its cost with the price of putting in several window units. You may discover that expensive as it is, the central unit turns out to be cheaper in the long run. If you decide to air-condition all or part of your building, once again, make the decision early in your planning. Even if your budget does not allow you to put in air conditioning immediately, the time to do any duct and electrical work is when the walls are already open, and not after they have been closed and wall-papered. In your planning, also be very careful about who you hire to evaluate and install the system. The air conditioning duct system must be carefully balanced so that the cooled air entering each room replaces an identical amount

Inside rooms, such as a kitchen or bathroom, must be ventilated to the outside.

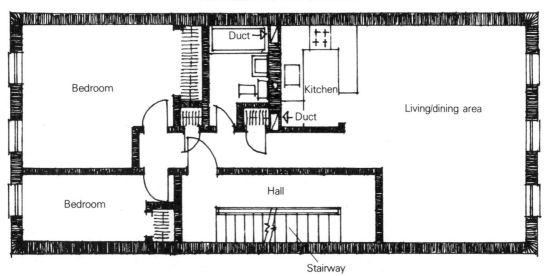

of warm air going to each unit. Placement of the duct registers, for example, has to be relatively precise so that the entire room they service is cooled.

MECHANICAL VENTILATION

Building codes regulate the amount of fresh air that every room in your house must receive. Some rooms, such as living rooms and sleeping areas, must have natural ventilation from windows; bathrooms, laundry rooms, and kitchens can be mechanically ventilated. Mechanical ventilation requires ducts that go from the room to the outside of the house; to circulate the necessary air there must also be a fan, which can be turned on separately or goes on automatically whenever the lights in the room are turned on. Or, there is a central fan on the roof controlled by a timer that switches it on periodically and allows it to run long enough to change the air in the rooms that are ducted to it. The system you use depends on your local building code, which, you will find, is very specific about the ducts, fan sizes, how they are installed, and the size of the rooms to be vented.

Mechanical ventilation can be a renovator's savior, particularly if you are dealing with a deep, narrow, urban row house with windows only in its front and back walls. Given a mechanical ventilation system, you can place the bathrooms, kitchens, and laundry rooms in the middle of such a house and use the windowed ends for living and sleeping rooms. But you must know exactly what your building code demands before you start building interior rooms, because the duct work will have to be hidden in some manner—presumably in the ceiling or up a wall somewhere; how you hide those ducts will have a lot to do with how you design the rooms.

3. Demolition and Rough Construction

WHETHER YOU ARE doing the work yourself or have hired a contractor, the first order of business is to remove all of the plaster, framing, molding, and floors that are to be replaced. Presumably, your general plan of the renovation tells you exactly what the bulk of the removal will be, including those areas that need to be opened up to make way for the electrical, plumbing, and heating lines.

Theoretically, everything in the house that must be removed should be taken out of the house at one time. But there are some exceptions to the rule. If you are living in the building while it is being renovated, it may be inconvenient to disassemble everything at the same time, particularly if the demolition is to include stairways and floors. Floors can actually be left for last—particularly if there is more than one to be removed—again, for the sake of convenience. Other items you ought to keep until their replacement is imminent are doors and windows. Even if the windows are drafty and the doors don't close very well, they do offer a certain amount of privacy and protection from the elements. So only take them out of their frames at the time you are about to install their replacements.

BEFORE YOU BEGIN

Some of the potential problems involved in demolition work can be avoided by paying close attention to this checklist:

1. Remove all hardware, mirrors, and everything else that might be broken or lost during the fury of pulling down the walls.

2. If you intend to save some items for reuse, either remove them or clearly mark them so they are not inadvertently thrown away.

3. When removing moldings and trim, or anything that might be reused elsewhere in the house, save them. Moldings around doors and windows fit into this category, and so do flooring and framing members. Old houses were constructed using studs that measure 2" x 4". Lumber is not made to those exact dimensions any more, and if you want to build new partition walls that are the same thickness as all the other walls in the house, the old framing members are easier (and a whole lot cheaper) to clean up and reuse than buying new wood, which will have to be widened with half-inch shims.

4. Any floors that are not to be removed must be protected from falling timbers, heavy machinery (such as pipe-cutting equipment your plumber is likely to bring with him), and falling plaster. Cover the floors with 15-lb. building paper and tape it down every foot or so. This goes for new floors as well—the moment they are laid, cover them until all the work is done and they can be given their finish coatings.

5. Unglazed tile of any sort absorbs dirt and liquids and should be sealed as soon as it is installed. Even so, tiled floors should be covered until the renovation is over.

6. New bathtubs, once they are installed, are climbed into and out of by the plumbers, plasterers, tilers, and painters. Even if you are doing the work of all those people, protect the tub with a plastic sheet or building paper.

7. Do not bring electrical fixtures or small hardware into the renovation area until it is time to install them. They can become lost or damaged if they are just lying around the work area for days or weeks.

8. Cover all items you do not want painted *before* any painting begins. Paint splatters in all directions, particularly if you are using a roller.

9. If you have hired workmen to come onto your renovation site, get your own tools out of the way. It is very easy for a workman to pack up the wrong tools when he is leaving, even if he honestly does not mean to steal them.

BEGIN AT THE TOP

When you are renovating anything, always start at the top and work down. If you are gutting an entire house part by part, start at the top floor, remove everything you want to remove, and then move down to the next floor. Pack up all of the debris and get it out of the house, then clean all of the rooms. Only then are you ready to begin any construction.

In some instances, the first order of business will be to do the wiring, heating, and plumbing work first. If there is any rough plumbing, such as installing a new soil stack or toilet bends, it should probably be done immediately. However, some rough carpentry work may have to be done in the kitchen, laundry room, and bathrooms before you can bring the plumbing lines into the rooms and position them exactly.

Electrical work is easiest to do when walls are open. If you plan to cut into the walls that will remain so that electrical lines can be snaked up from the basement to the top floor (and no electricity is to be placed in any of the new walls you intend to erect), the electrical work can begin as soon as the debris has been removed. Otherwise, wait until the framing in your renovation area has been completed before you begin snaking cables through the house.

If it will be necessary to extend the heating system, you can have the pipes carried into the new rooms before they are built, but once again, the exact positioning of radiators may depend on where your new walls will stand, and it might be better to at least frame those walls before the heating experts do any work.

When you're finally ready to begin the actual demolition, your first step is to pull down the ceiling (on the top floor first, if you're working on two or more stories). Then you must knock out whatever walls are destined for the rubbish heap. If one particular room is to be renovated immediately, take up its flooring as soon as the debris from the ceiling and walls is cleaned up.

Take note of the fact that any degree of demolition, from removing the smallest wall to tearing out the innards of an entire floor, is a messy, dusty, miserable job. Furthermore, it is noisy and time consuming. Actually, pulling down plaster and knocking out framing members are easy, compared to removing the rubbish afterwards. You can knock down an average-sized wall in about 30 minutes; it will take the rest of the day to get rid of the plaster and wood that pile up around you.

Some Tips on Pulling Down Plaster

No matter what part of a house you are demolishing, if plaster is involved the entire building will get dirty, since plaster dust is a very fine powder that gets up in the air quickly and takes time to settle. It is also hard to wash off your walls, floors, and furniture because the moment you touch it with a damp rag it starts leaving streaks. You can assume it will take several thorough housecleanings before all of the dust is washed out of the farthest corners of the house. Plaster is something that cannot be demolished without making a tremendous mess, and you simply have to resign yourself to the chore of cleaning it up.

How you go about that cleanup job is often determined by the rules enforced in your neighborhood, along with the size of the job you have to tackle. If you are only removing a plaster ceiling, you may be able to pack the plaster in boxes (it is too heavy for plastic garbage bags to hold) and stack the boxes outside to be taken away during normal garbage collection. There is an old trick to pulling down plaster ceilings that you might consider:

1. Cover the floor under the ceiling with open cardboard boxes. The boxes should be wedged tightly together and cover every inch of the floor.

2. Put your ladder legs in the boxes as you work and pull down the plaster.

3. During demolition, most of the plaster and lath will fall into the boxes.

4. When the ceiling is clean, you can fill half-empty boxes from other boxes that are less full, tie them up, and get rid of them. You will save yourself considerable work and reduce the plaster dust in the air, since much of it will be trapped between the sides of the boxes when the plaster falls.

When you go at a major removal project, you may find that the best way of efficiently getting rid of the debris is with dumpsters. Dumpsters are those big iron boxes you see parked in the gutter from time to time. You can find them in the yellow pages of your telephone book. It costs about $100 to have one delivered to your doorstep and then taken away in about three days. If you rent one, you can throw things into it from the front windows, but the easiest way of filling it is to build a long trough-slide out of canvas or wood that extends from the dumpster to one of your windows.

CONSTRUCTION WORK

Your renovation falls into two general categories, **rough** and **finish**. The rough portion includes all work that must go on inside the walls, ceilings, and floors, including plumbing and electrical lines, heating pipes, ducts, flues, and framing. The finish work begins when you close up

the walls, and includes installation of the doors and windows, molding, trim, flooring, painting, and wallcovering.

The rough work comes first. It is easiest, but not always practical, to do all of the rough work before any of the finishing begins. But if you are redoing an entire house, there may be a point, after the plumbing, electrical, heating, and duct work is done, when it is more reasonable to complete one floor at a time. Or perhaps certain rooms, such as the kitchen or a bathroom, can be completed before you do the rest of the house. In any case, the rough work should be pretty much completed all over the building before you go on to the more delicate procedures of finishing work.

THE ROUGH WORK

Given the complications of rough plumbing and the local building code's standards for electrical work, some plumbing and electrical work might have to be done by professionals. For the sake of your budget, however, try to keep the amount of labor they do to a minimum. There is nothing difficult about snaking electrical cables through walls and bringing them to the distribution panel. Nor is there any great difficulty in making the drain connections between a soil stack and the fixtures, or even installing the fixtures. What you may need a plumber for is to complete the heating lines and/or put up the soil stack, as well as to do whatever work is required for the gas lines. Most communities demand that a licensed electrician install the distribution panel and hook up the circuit breakers.

As for rough carpentry, even if you have never before framed a wall, the only difficulty you face is in making certain the wall goes exactly where you want it to go. Your three best friends as a rough carpenter are a 2-foot spirit level, a folding carpenter's rule, and a roofing square. Every joint between members must be at a right angle, and all members must be level and vertical, as well as exactly 16" or 24" on center (o.c.). "On center" means the distance from the middle of one stud

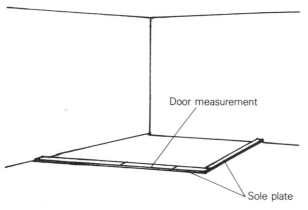

Nail the sole plate in place first.

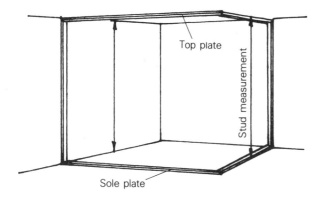

Install one wall stud and use it to get the top plate plumb over the sole plate.

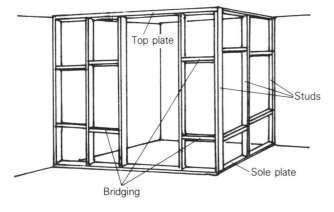

Bridging between studs can be judiciously placed to coincide with shelves or poles that must be supported inside the closet.

to the middle of the adjacent stud. Trying to get every stud exactly spaced can be a chore. The wood tends to be driven out of line as you pound nails diagonally through its ends, and the studs wind up standing crooked. Here are some secrets of assembling a frame of any sort that have been quietly passed by word of mouth between do-it-yourself renovators for years:

1. When you are working alone, as many renovators do, it is almost impossible to control your studs and keep them in line as you nail them. One way to make the nailing easier is to drill pilot holes diagonally through each side of the stud ends. You do this by drilling half an inch straight into the wood, then back the drill out and enter the same hole at a 45° angle toward the end of the wood. Since studs should be nailed on all four sides, drill holes in each side, using a $1/32''$ drill or any size that is less than a third of the diameter of the nail shaft.

2. A second way of making your studs fall exactly on center is to cut a piece of $2'' \times 4''$ lumber exactly $14\frac{1}{2}''$ long and use it as a spacer. Once you have installed the first stud, presumably against the wall, your partition will intersect; lay the spacer against it and stand the next stud against its end. Drive your first nail into the side of the new stud that is opposite the spacer, then place the two edge nails. Remove the spacer and hit the last nail into the stud.

3. Old houses are notoriously out of square. Rarely is there an absolutely right-angle corner anywhere to be found. Moreover, the floors and ceilings are almost never parallel. You can begin a new wall at one end, where it is 9 feet-6" high and discover it is 9 feet-11" at the other side of the house. Or it may be 9 feet-6" at the far wall, but 9 feet-11" in the middle somewhere. The safest procedure is, unfortunately, the slowest:

a.) Position the sole plate exactly where you want the wall to run and nail it to the floor.

b.) Stand a stud up against whatever wall the partition is to intersect and make certain it is plumb, then nail it in place (or bolt it with lag bolts and lead plugs if you are attaching to masonry). Be sure the top of the stud is $1\frac{1}{2}''$ shorter than the ceiling, so you can fit the top plate between it and the ceiling.

c.) If the partition extends to another wall, stand a second stud up on the sole plate and make it level against the opposite wall.

d.) If the partition ends partway across the room, measure the distance from the ceiling to the sole plate and cut a stud 1½" shorter than your measurement.

e.) Now cut a top plate, the exact length as the sole plate.

f.) If you have the two studs standing, jam the top plate against the ceiling between them.

g.) If the partition is a partial wall, nail your second stud to the top plate and stand it up on the end of the sole plate, jamming the free end of the top plate under the wall stud.

h.) Before you nail anything, make certain the top plate is absolutely plumb with the sole plate.

i.) Technically, walls should have two top plates. The second plate can be nailed to the underside of the top plate you have attached to the ceiling and toe-nailed into the end studs.

j.) All of the other studs in the wall are then measured separately at their proper positions and installed.

4. Remember, there must be a wood surface at least ¾" wide for every edge of the wall surface material. The places where those surfaces are hard to come by are the corners not only between walls, but between walls and ceilings as well. You may find that some edges need to be given a 1" × 2" furring strip nailed to the side of a stud, so that the edge of a wallboard panel has something it can attach to. (See next page.)

5. Hanging a door is, under all but optimum conditions, a time-consuming business; it can take four or five hours to put a new door in an old frame and make it work properly. "Optimum conditions" occur when you build the door frame and attach the jack studs to the hinge side of the frame. Then nail the jambs to the hinge side and header, and hang the door. When the door is in place, position the latch-side jack stud and jamb exactly where you want them and nail them in position. If they don't quite touch the frame stud, fill the gap with shims.

Anatomy of a door and a window frame

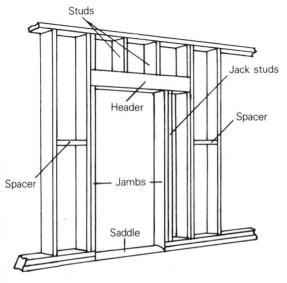

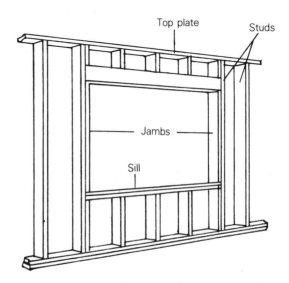

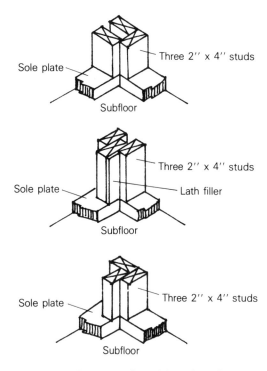

Three approved ways of making framing corners

After Framing

After your framing is complete, when all the walls and ceilings are in place, hang whatever electrical cables are necessary and install the switches and outlets, attaching the electrical boxes to studs or between joists.

If the floor requires any work that calls for removing the floorboards, do it before the walls are framed. A badly tilted floor that needs to be leveled must have the floorboards removed so that the joists can be shimmed or replaced, as the case may be. If you intend to put down a new floor, make your subfloor from ¾" plywood panels, but *do not* put down the flooring until the walls and ceilings have been covered. If it is not necessary to remove the flooring, whatever you do to it can be done at a later time.

Anatomy of a modern floor. Old houses often do not have a subfloor. If you go down to the joists, put the subfloor in before laying your new flooring.

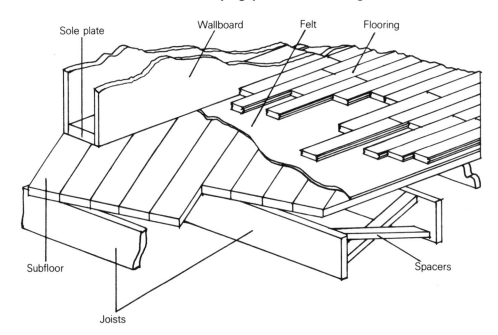

4. Closing the Walls and Ceilings

THE WALLS AND CEILINGS of old houses are almost always made of plaster and lath. Some people think old plaster is precious and should be preserved; if it happens to be in good condition, it might as well be. But the original purpose of the plaster was to present a smooth, flat surface, and this it has done for upward of 50 years while the house has settled, while people have hammered picture hooks in it, and while the building has endured many cold winters and steamy summers. Now the plaster has cracks in it, both large and small. But far more important than the looks of it, all that lath that holds the plaster in place has dried out.

Lath is a series of rough-hewn wooden strips half an inch thick and an inch wide, spaced half an inch apart across the studs and joists. They are made of pine or fir and over the past decades they have lost all of their original moisture. They have lost so much moisture they are now eminently suitable as tinder for starting fires. If there is ever a fire in your lovely old renovation, and flames get inside one of the walls, the fire will travel up that lath with astounding speed. It will take less than five minutes to burn its way up three stories and lick through the roof, and within an hour that kind of fire can gut the entire building. The lath behind all of your plaster is tantamount to a fused bomb that needs nothing more than a match to set it off.

Don't tear out all the plaster walls in your house; it is more work than it is worth. But any-time you have occasion to replace a wall or build a new one, don't be pigheaded about using plaster. In the first place, plaster is difficult to apply on a large surface and get smooth. The odds are you will have to hire a plasterer to do the work, and because plasterers are an endangered species, they are expensive. Secondly, you can use wallboard (or Sheetrock, plasterboard, gypsumboard—they are all the same thing) and get it up in half the time with half the hassle, and it will not present nearly the fire hazard.

Old wooden lath is nailed to the studs and joists and used to hold plaster walls and ceilings in place. If you are repairing a crack or hole in the plaster, use a chisel to undercut the edges of the area to help the new plaster hold.

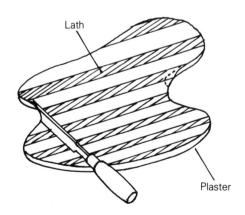

Lath

Plaster

But Plaster You Must

If there are any original walls or ceilings to be left in your old house, the odds are you will have to do some sort of plastering somewhere. Working with plaster is tricky because the material hardens very quickly, so you do not have much time to get it smooth before it dries. Bearing that fact in mind, try to keep the areas you have to patch down to a minimum size and always consider using some material other than plaster of paris, such as spackle or wallboard compound.

If you must use plaster to fill in a hole, the area should be cleared of all old, loose plaster and then thoroughly soaked in water. Fresh plaster does not adhere well to old plaster, so add a bonding agent to your mixture.

In areas that are missing lath, you can back the space with any of several products, including metal mesh, wallboard, or plasterboard. If you want to keep your plastering to a minimum, use the plasterboard and cut it to fit tightly against the edges of the hole. Build it up to a fraction of an inch below the surface of the wall; then cover it with spackle, plaster, or joint compound.

It is virtually impossible to smooth a wall filled with hairline cracks. You can fill the cracks or

A piece of wire mesh can be used to fill a hole that has no lath behind it. Keep the mesh in place by tying it to a stick until the first coat of plaster has hardened, then remove the stick.

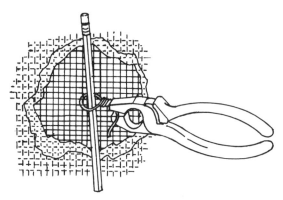

cover them with just about anything, and they will still come back to haunt you. The obvious solution is to knock down the wall and replace the plaster with wallboard, but you might also be able to get away with nailing the wallboard to the plaster, or even gluing it there with joint compound.

DECORATIVE MOLDINGS AND MEDALLIONS

The moldings around the edges of your ceiling are very likely made of plaster. Typically, they were manufactured as individual units and then positioned in place with plaster when the ceiling was constructed. The moldings are in segments, and sometimes the seams between sections are visible.

Most medallions were manufactured as one piece, and are therefore very heavy. Usually, metal rods or wires are embedded in the underside of the medallion; these combine with the plaster to hold the medallion in position against the ceiling. By working carefully around the perimeter of a medallion, you can pull it off the ceiling after its tie-rods have been freed from the joists, and position it elsewhere, if you wish. Broken or missing medallions can be replaced with facsimiles manufactured from a new synthetic material called anaglupta. These are inexpensive and light enough to glue to the ceiling, but they are reproductions.

Parts of decorative molding are always missing in an old house. Sometimes it is just a small section, but often whole chunks of it are gone. If the configuration of the molding is simple, you may be able to find pieces of wooden molding which, when you nail them together, will look enough like the plaster so that no one notices the difference when it is up on the ceiling and painted.

If the wood-on-the-ceiling trick doesn't work, or if it offends your sense of history, you can try making a "cast" of plaster and creating your own section to fill in the gaps in the molding:

1. Clean the damaged area of the molding of all loose plaster and coat it with a bonding agent.

2. Coat a good section of molding with vegetable oil. Get the oil on both the wall below the molding and the ceiling beside it.

3. Mix some plaster, and pile it on a piece of wood that is longer than the damaged area.

4. Press the plaster against the oil-coated portion of the molding, trying to get some of it against the wall and ceiling on either side of the molding. Slide the board back and forth while pressing it against the molding.

5. When the plaster has hardened enough to hold its shape, remove it and allow it to dry thoroughly.

6. Coat the inside of your cast with vegetable oil.

7. Fill the damaged area of the molding with wet plaster.

8. Push the cast into the plaster and slide it back and forth over the wet material. If you have made the cast large enough to touch the ceiling and wall, you will have better control of it. In fact, with a little practice, you can create patches in your molding that hardly show, once they have been painted.

9. Remove the cast when the plaster under it is hard enough to hold its shape, and scrape away any excess plaster around your patch before it has a chance to completely harden.

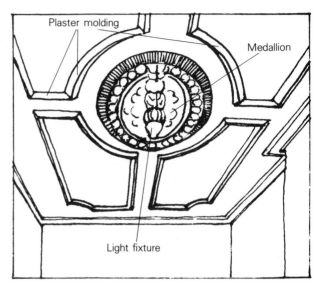

Medallions can be taken off a ceiling and replaced.

One way to get around a broken medallion is to remove it, but then you must outline its area with molding.

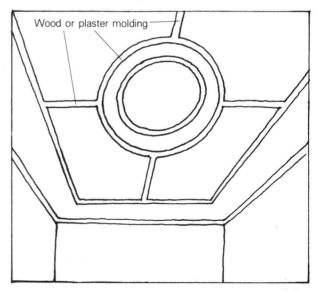

WORKING WITH WALLBOARD

Wallboard is sold in panels that measure 4 feet by 8, 10, 12, and 16 feet, and are ½", ⅜", or ⅝" thick. Wallboard is known by many names, including Sheetrock, plasterboard, gypsumboard, and drywall. It consists of plaster sandwiched between sheets of heavy paper, and therefore each panel is not only cumbersome, but heavy. The idea of the panels, which offer a variety of edges including a tongue-and-groove version, is that they will fit across 16" or 24" o.c. studs or joists, with their outer edges landing along the center

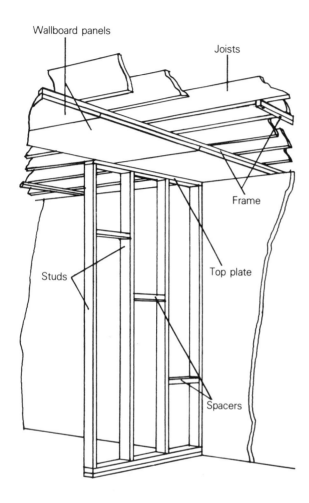

Wallboard panels

Joists

Frame

Studs

Top plate

Spacers

Always install wallboard on the ceiling before the walls.

bodily harm to yourself. The important point to remember about any wallboard is that it must be fully supported. If you are nailing ⅝" material to studs, the studs can be 24" apart (o.c.). But ½" and ⅜" wallboard must be supported every 16" o.c. Under normal conditions, the different thicknesses are used in this manner:

- Walls: ⅜" or ⅝"
- Ceilings: ½"

There is also a waterproof version of wallboard that is green because of the chemicals coating the paper. This is manufactured in all panel sizes, but is only a half-inch thick and is applied to all walls that might be subjected to moisture. This means that the walls behind any sink, and usually all of the walls and ceilings in bathrooms, should be covered with it.

Some Tips on Putting Up Wallboard

1. When you are nailing a wallboard panel, begin along the center stud or joist. Believe it or not, you can get bulges in a panel if you start nailing at the edges.

2. Place groups of two nails 6" apart along all edges. The double-nailing procedure is a guarantee that nails will not pop later.

3. On occasion, people install double thicknesses of wallboard, primarily to reduce sound and help insulate the room. If you are doing an entire wall this way, stand the first layer of panels vertically; nail the second layer horizontally, so the joints never coincide.

4. The standard notion about wallboard panels is that they are supposed to stand with their long sides running from the floor to the ceiling. But there are times when placing the panels that way creates more joints than if they were used horizontally. Generally speaking, put up your panels in any way that will leave the fewest joints.

5. When you are wallboarding an entire room, put the ceiling up first, so that the wall panels can come up under the edges and help hold the ceiling panels in place.

line of the framing members. They will do this unerringly, so long as your studs or joists are placed 16" or 24" on center. If one of the edge studs is off by more than ¾", however, the panel edge will have nothing to attach to.

Wallboard panels are, relatively speaking, delicate. They can stand for years against a proper frame, but not by themselves; you can, in fact, stick your fist through one without doing any

6. Getting a 4- × 8-foot × ½″ wallboard panel up to the joists over a 10-foot ceiling is no picnic, and is almost impossible for one person to accomplish alone—unless you have a platform you can raise and lower. Even with two men working, once the panel is up against the joists, it is mean work holding the panel up while driving in the first half-dozen nails.

An invaluable assist in holding ceiling panels in place so they can be nailed is known as the **panel brace.** It is made by nailing a 1″ × 6″ board 4 feet long to the end of a 2″ × 4″ to form a T. The 2″ × 4″ is cut slightly longer than the height of the room. As soon as the panel is against the ceiling, the brace can be rammed up against it and will hold it until your nailing is completed.

7. Put up all the wallboard in the area you are covering before you begin taping the joints.

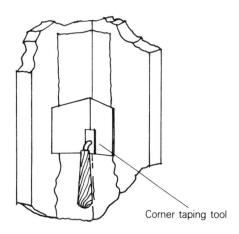

Corner taping tool

You can buy corner-taping tools that make getting into corners with joint compound a whole lot easier.

A wallboard panel brace is made by nailing a 1″ x 6″ board to the end of a length of 2″ x 4″ cut to the height of the room.

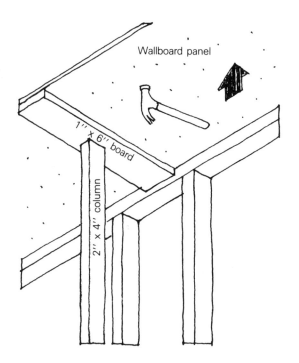

Wallboard panel

1″ x 6″ board

2″ x 4″ column

The processes are totally different and require different tools, so it is easier to complete one phase of the job before you go on to the next.

8. Taping is dull work and there are no machines that can help you; the best way to get the taping finished is to have lots of people doing it. Mistakes can easily be sanded off or filled in.

9. When you are applying joint compound over tape, don't try to do the job with one thick coating. Wallboard manufacturers recommend three thin, smooth applications, each one feathering farther out from the tape.

NEW MOLDING AND TRIM

When the wall joints are covered and smoothed, and the doors are hung with their stops in place, the next step is to install molding around the doors and windows, in the corners between walls and ceiling, and nail baseboards along the floor.

There is not much to do with molding, other than cut it to the correct lengths and nail it in

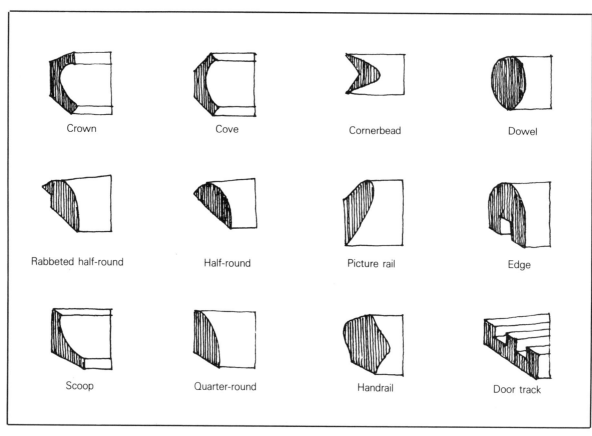

Crown	Cove	Cornerbead	Dowel
Rabbeted half-round	Half-round	Picture rail	Edge
Scoop	Quarter-round	Handrail	Door track

Some of the common molding configurations available at lumber yards

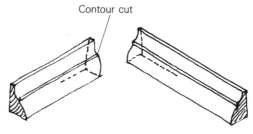

Miter joint

45° angle

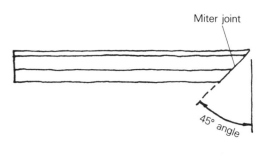

Contour cut

Molding, trim, and baseboards should meet at miter joints.

place. The molding around doors and windows should be lined up along the edges of the jambs and end ¼" from the inside edge. That is, it covers half an inch of a ¾"-thick jamb, and extends over the joints between the jambs and the wall facing. If you are reinstalling old molding that has been in the room, or molding that comes from elsewhere in the house, ask yourself if it is ready to accept whatever decorative materials will go over it. A good time to strip the paint from molding is before it is installed; if it is old wood with plenty of curves and grooves, probably the best way of removing the paint (certainly the easiest way) is to send it out to a lye bath.

If the molding is fresh from your neighborhood lumber yard, you may want to give it a primer coat of paint before you install it.

The only problem that may arise with molding is a mental one. Molding should meet at all corners in a miter joint. That means the ends of the pieces entering a corner must be cut at a 45° angle, which may not sound difficult, but sometimes it is. Crown molding, in particular, is likely to have a multiple-curved front surface and some strange angles along its back so that it can fit diagonally between the top of the wall and the edge of the ceiling. No matter what saw you are using (a radial arm is best, but a backsaw and miter box will do almost as well) the problem is to find which of the many angled surfaces should be rested on the saw table, and which on the back guard. But once you have figured out how to hold the molding, all you know is how to hold it for cutting one side of the joint. The opposing side will have to be held in the opposite direction. Then when you come to outside corners, everything has to be turned over, or around, until you find out how *those* angles are cut. You will save yourself a lot of headaches if you buy an extra piece of molding and spend whatever time it takes to figure out how it must be cut. At 28 cents a running foot for crown molding, you hardly want to start wasting 10-foot pieces by cutting wrong angles.

Baseboards are installed in the same manner as molding, with finishing nails that are countersunk and covered with wood putty. Molding can be nailed anywhere there is a framing member to go into. Baseboards should be nailed along the bottom edge, with every other nail entering the floor and the wall sole plate. Pin the top of the baseboard to the wall at every other stud. However, you may not want to install the baseboards until after you have prepared the floor.

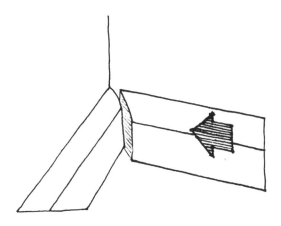

Fitting mitered baseboards into an inside corner

Nail a baseboard to both the wall and the floor, as well as at any outside corners. The nails should be countersunk and then covered with wood putty.

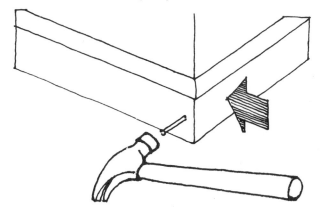

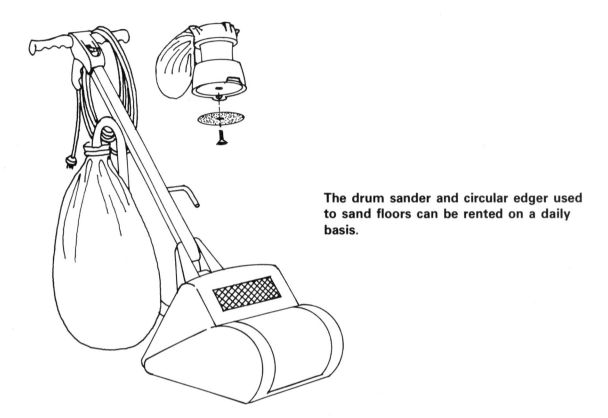

The drum sander and circular edger used to sand floors can be rented on a daily basis.

Underlayment must be nailed 4″ to 6″ in all directions.

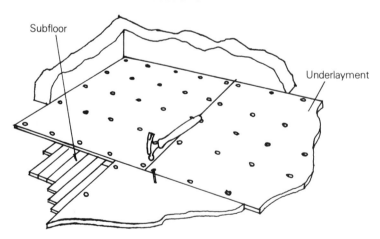

Subfloor

Underlayment

FLOORING

If you are laying a new floor, the old floor should be removed and the new subflooring panels laid before any walls are erected. The new floor itself should be installed before the baseboards are put in place, so that the boards can cover the edges of the flooring.

If you intend to put parquet squares or resilient flooring over the original floor, an underlayment must first be nailed down to even the old floor and provide a smooth gluing surface for the squares. The underlayment can be as thin as ¼" hardboard or chipboard panels, if the old floor is relatively even. If there are gaps or large cracks in the old floor, or if the floor is more like a roller-coaster than a slide, use ½" or even ¾" press-board or plywood. The underlayment *must* be nailed solidly in place. Nails should be driven through it every 4" to 6" in all directions, and the joint between panels should be tight. When you finish nailing the panels, walk all over them and drive nails into any area that squeaks or gives. If the underlayment is not solidly down on the floor, it will cause the finish flooring to work loose.

If the existing floor is in good shape and needs only to be sanded and finished, do the sanding before you paint or wallpaper the rest of the room. The process of sanding a floor requires two large sanding machines which you can rent from a neighborhood hardware store (see the yellow pages of your telephone directory). You can sand down the entire floor of an average urban row house, and even get the first coats of polyurethane on it, in less than a day. But the dust that rises from the sanding will cling to everything in the room, including fresh paint.

You may not want to polyurethane the floor before you paint or wallpaper the rest of the room, but it should be stained as soon as it is sanded or the wood grain will rise and you'll have to sand the floor again. The best approach is to stain and apply the sander-filler to the floor, then cover it with plastic sheeting until you are ready to apply the polyurethane. You can attach the baseboards once the floor has been sanded. The big sanding machines tend to leave about a quarter of an inch of unsanded wood along the walls, which the baseboards will effectively cover.

With the proper finishing touches and decor, you can make the long, narrow parlor of an urban row house look very contemporary.

If antique molding, a fireplace, and other original details are preserved, the parlor floor of an urban row house can be modern and still historical in atmosphere.

5. Finishing Details

WHEN YOU REMOVE parts of the inside of a house and then replace them with new walls and ceilings, there is a point when you can step into any room and it looks just like any other room in the world, let alone in the rest of the house. In theory, it has square walls and a ceiling that is more or less parallel with the floor, a door or two, and maybe a few windows. It is a box, and as such is not particularly distinguished until the finishing details are added. The trim around the ceiling, the type of doors and windows and the molding that surrounds those units, the color of the ceiling, the print of the wallpaper, the type of hardware that decorates the doors—anything, in fact, that will be visible in any room comes under the heading of **finishing work;** and because it is visible, every material should be chosen carefully with an eye toward its contribution to the overall look of the room.

Every finishing detail must also be meticulously installed to make so perfect an appearance that nobody ever notices any traces of the installation. That means that the doors on cabinets must hang parallel to each other; that the joints between pieces of molding should be no more visible than a thin joining line in the corners; that there are no bumps in the walls, and so on. You can frame the four walls of a room in a day and wallboard them in another day, and complete taping them in a third. You can then take weeks to complete all of the finishing details. There is very little room for error in any of the finishing work, i.e., there is no space for impatience or hastiness.

WINDOWS

Windows are a part of most rooms. In an old house windows can be all sorts of dimensions and configurations, and by the time you acquire the house they can also be very old, and very

You can stop a considerable amount of air leakage with weatherstripping.

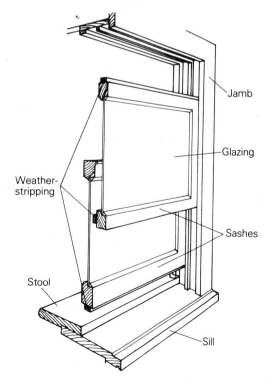

Jamb

Glazing

Weather-stripping

Sashes

Stool

Sill

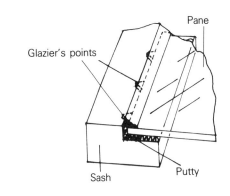

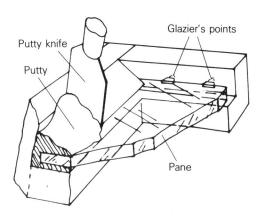

When replacing glass, clear out the rabbet in the frame and muntins, then place a roll of putty in the grooves to support the glass and pin the pane in place with glazier's points. The putty along the outside edge of the glass should be angled at 45°.

leaky, and not at all energy-efficient. You may be able to repair the sashes and reputty the panes to make them airtight, and then protect them with storm windows. You may also find that it is less time consuming and more energy-efficient to replace the windows altogether.

New windows cost money—especially the kind that are 3 feet wide and about 8 feet high, usually found in the parlors of urban row houses. Double-hung windows, which have upper and lower sashes, are categorized according to the number of panes in each sash: they are called one-over-one; two-over-two; four-over-four; six-over-six; or four-over-one, and so on. All of these

can be reproduced by window manufacturers in single-, double-, and even triple- and quadruple-paned units.

When you decide to replace the windows in your house, the major consideration, beyond improving the energy-efficiency of the units, is the way they look. Obviously, it's your house, so if you want to replace those six-over-six front windows, go ahead. But if you mean to maintain the architectural integrity of the house, your best choice of replacement unit is one that is similar, if not identical, to the type you now have. Architecturally speaking, houses that were designed with sashed windows do not look very well with casements, or jalousies, in their place. You can get away with changing the number of panes in each sash. For example, the twelve-over-twelve might be changed to six-over-six or even one-over-one. (However, one-over-one windows may not look appropriate to the building—at least on its more public sides.) In any case, the more panes there are in each sash, the harder it is to clean the window.

Still, it may be desirable to change your old windows with a casement or even a plate-glass window; if it is going in the back wall and overlooks the garden, it will enhance the view of your backyard or bring more light into the kitchen—even though the design may be an aesthetic no-no.

If you are replacing the windows in your renovation, once you have opted for the most architecturally compatible design, look for the most energy-efficient unit you can find. It is possible to buy quadruple-paned windows, but they are more expensive than triple panes, so there comes a point where the cost of the windows is not justified by the amount of fuel they will save. If you are changing a dozen large windows, you can get into a cost of $200 or $300 apiece just for the double-glazed units, which are quite energy-efficient.

Not very efficient, of course, are single-paned windows, so with them you also need storms. Storm windows plus the new single-paned units can cost more than double-glazed units, so you

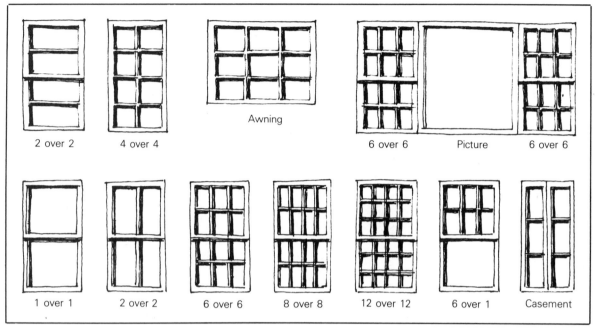

Window types found in older houses

Modern, large-paned windows seldom look well in an old house.

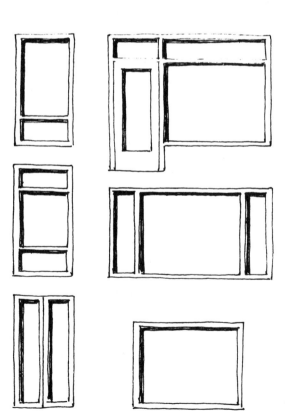

have to be careful about making a cost analysis of your windows.

Installing a replacement window is a time-consuming but not terribly demanding chore. The windows, particularly in an old house, are very likely not a standard size, so they must be custom made. If at all possible, have the window manufacturer's representative measure the windows for you; that way, if there are any mistakes you won't have to pay for them. The windows will be delivered to you complete with frames. You'll have to remove the old sashes and jambs, and get the hole down to its framing members, and then put the new unit in place and shim it wherever necessary to get it level and plumb. It does take some time to line each window up, and you can reckon on installing about two a day if you are working alone.

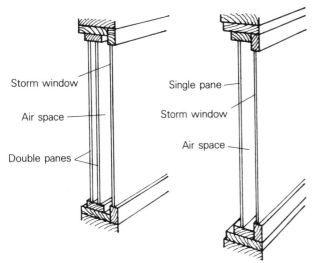

Storm window

Air space

Double panes

Single pane

Storm window

Air space

Double-paned windows are quite energy-efficient, especially when supplemented by a storm window. For single-paned windows, storms are a must.

SHUTTERS

Many urban row houses built around the turn of the twentieth century were designed with shutter wells on either side of the windows, to allow heavy wooden shutters to fold back out of the way, if not practically out of sight. Sometimes the shutters are missing; sometimes they are stuck in the walls, and it seems like they are missing when they are really just recessed.

Old shutters are prized by many renovators, and people go to great lengths to strip them of the fifty years of paint that cover them, salvage or install new hardware on them, and get them working again. If there is a missing shutter or two, you have to hang around the neighborhood until you can find a similar old unit to use as a replacement. What you cannot do is run around the corner to your neighborhood lumberyard and buy a replacement. Nobody makes heavy-weight shutters the way they used to, and the modern shutters are not compatible to the old ones in any way. If you are missing one or two shutters, you may be able to find an old discard and fill in the hole. If you have entire windows to fill, you can do it with modern-made wooden shutters, but

they are lighter in appearance and do not hide the fact that they are modern, even if you artfully paint or stain them.

Painting and staining shutters is a long chore, because every little slat has six tiny sides that have to be covered. Removing years of paint from a shutter is even more time consuming. The best way—really the only way—to clean old shutters of their finish coating is to send them out to a lye bath, or make your own lye tub and do it yourself. But trying to hand-strip one shutter, let alone 48 of them, can become a lifetime occupation that isn't worth the effort.

DOORS

The replacement of doors is less expensive and easier to accomplish than changing windows. Stock doors are sold in a range of widths and heights, and in thicknesses of either 1⅜" or 1¾". Most doors are between 6 feet-8" and 7 feet in height, and exterior doors are always 1¾" thick.

There are two types of doors, **flush** and **paneled**. Flush doors have flat sides and may be hollow or solid cored. Paneled doors have panels inserted inside a frame construction of wood, glass, or any number of other materials. Most likely, you can find a door that looks very much like the doors in the rest of the building. When you are installing doors in the new portions of a renovation, be consistent throughout the floor. The decorative molding and trim, the type of windows, and the doors should be harmonious throughout the entire floor of a house, even if they present a different appearance than some of the other floors.

One way you can "fake it" with your doors is to buy inexpensive hollow doors (they are half the price of any other door type) and then decorate them with strips of molding. The strips can be purchased in lengths and cut to size, or in kits of pre-cut moldings that are glued to the face of the unit.

Old doors can almost always be repaired if they are split or have broken rails or styles. But the most common problem with old doors is a chewed-up hinge edge. The door, particularly if it is solid, has probably had its hinges changed a dozen times since it was first installed. Not only is the door edge in poor condition, but the hinge jamb on the door frame will be just as bad. If the jamb is really a mess, exchange it for a new piece of wood—it is only a piece of 1" × 5". However, the molding can also be in poor condition, and that may not be so easy to replace. Try to hide the damaged portions behind the hinges and with the dexterous use of wood putty.

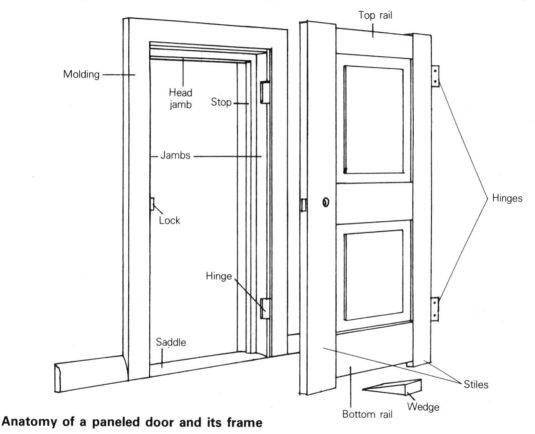

Anatomy of a paneled door and its frame

The five steps to mortising a hinge. Make the mortise only as deep as the thickness of the hinge leaf.

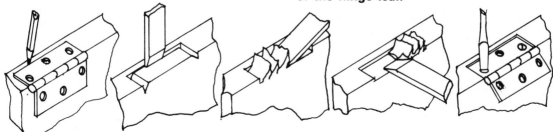

To hide the damage in a door edge, cut out the area and replace it with a straight piece of wood that is glued and doweled, or glue and screwed into place. If the new hinges are to go into the replacement blocks, make them as large as possible, perhaps long enough to extend from hinge to hinge.

Doors are normally easier to strip than shutters or molding, but it is still easier to have them lye-dipped than to expend the energy taking down many coats of paint with a chemical stripper.

DOOR AND WINDOW MOLDING

The rule of current architectural and decorating taste dictates that all the molding around the doors and windows of a room must be the same.

A door or window can look dramatically different merely by changing the molding around its frame.

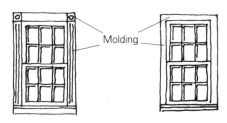

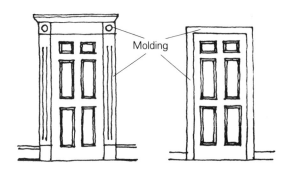

New wallboard ceiling (no frame)

Sometimes you can nail wallboard panels directly to the old ceiling.

It is a tough rule to break without having parts of the room looking a little weird, so if you are installing a new door somewhere and do not have the right molding to surround it, you ought to replace all of the molding in the room.

The jamb molding should end ¼" back from the face of the jamb in all cases, and, of course, it should cover the space between the frame and the wall surfacing.

CEILINGS

If a ceiling is beyond repair, you face the possibility of removing the plaster or wallboard attached to the joists and replacing it with new wallboard panels, or lowering the ceiling a few inches by constructing a frame made up of 2" × 4" joists and headers. Occasionally, you may be able to nail the new joists to the ceiling itself—provided you can drive your nails into the existing joists, in which case you may be able to use 1" × 2" furring strips. However, the molding around the rooms in old houses often extends way down the wall, and just tacking wallboard to the ceiling may leave a strange-looking union between your new ceiling and the old molding.

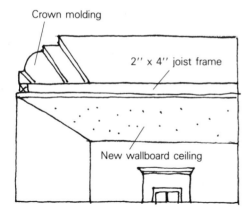

Crown molding

2'' x 4'' joist frame

New wallboard ceiling

If the crown molding is large, a new ceiling will have to be suspended from a 2'' x 4'' frame.

Usually, the easiest approach is to erect a ceiling frame that traverses the room just under the bottom of the crown molding. You do this by determining the height of the ceiling after taking measurements from the floor at several points along each wall. If the house is in any way off square (and it probably is), take the shortest height and mark it on the wall. Then draw a level line the length of the wall. The line has to be leveled with a carpenter's level and will have no parallel relationship with either the floor or the ceiling. If you continue your level line around the top of all the walls in the room, it should meet itself at your starting point, but it may very well look crooked in relation to the bottom of the crown molding.

Evaluate your level ceiling line. If the room has really gone askew, a level ceiling might well make the windows and doors look unacceptably out of whack and force you to strike some sort of off-level compromise for your ceiling. When you have determined the position of your ceiling, nail 2" × 4" or 2" × 3" lengths of stock to the walls, aligning each piece with your ceiling line. Try to use only one piece of wood for each wall, and nail it into every stud it crosses. When the frame is in place, toe-nail your joists 16" o.c. across the narrowest width of the room, then attach wallboard panels to them.

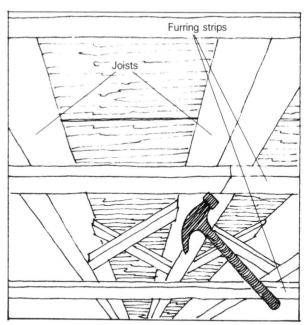

Furring strips

Joists

Light ceiling panels or squares can be attached to a furring-strip frame nailed to the ceiling or joists.

Ceiling tiles can be nailed or stapled in position.

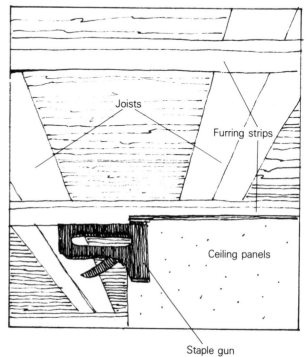

Joists

Furring strips

Ceiling panels

Staple gun

If your new ceiling is to be made of ceiling tiles, which are extremely light, they can be nailed or stapled to a furring-strip frame, rather than 2" × 4" or 2" × 3" boards. However, the strips have to be assembled according to the length and width of the tiles, or squares, which may be more like 12" square or 12" × 24".

Lowered ceilings that are designed to hide lighting fixtures must be placed at least 12" below the original ceiling to allow enough space for air to circulate around the heated lamps. The metal frame and panel materials that make up this type of ceiling all come with complete installation instructions, which should be followed closely.

Header strips as well as studs must be installed to support every edge of each panel. The studs should be 16'' o.c.

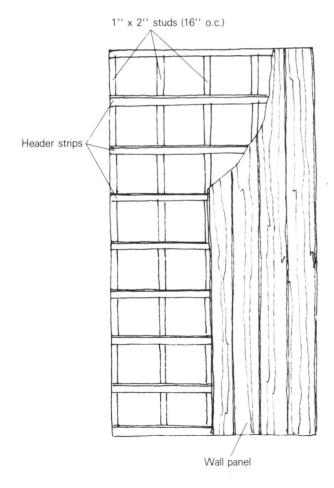

1'' x 2'' studs (16'' o.c.)

Header strips

Wall panel

WALLS

Standard plaster-and-lath or wallboard walls are ready to be painted or wallpapered when they have been smoothed and all cracks and holes have been properly filled. If you have a wall, or even a room, that has uncommonly poor plaster, the easiest way of covering it may be to install one of the many types of wood panels available on today's market. The panels range from ¾" down to ⅛" thick, and can be manufactured out of almost any material from real wood to laminated plastic. Generally, they are sold in 4- × 8-foot panels that must be glued and/or nailed to a furring-strip frame, which, in turn, is nailed directly to the wall.

Header strips should be nailed across the top and bottom of the wall, although you can use the existing baseboard as the bottom header in many cases. The studs are then placed every 16" o.c., hopefully nailing into the wall studs behind them. If the wall studs are not in the right place, you may have to anchor the furring strips with molly or toggle bolts. Whatever you do, make sure that a strip is positioned behind every edge of every panel and that all joints between panels can be made over a firm wooden backing.

Rather than try to cut the paneling to fit exactly around the door and window molding, remove the molding before you install your panels. Then carry the panels as far as the door or window jambs, and nail the molding back over it. You will save a lot of time and gain a neater appearance around all of the room's apertures.

Insulate Before You Panel. If you are paneling an outside wall that has no insulation in it, consider framing the wall with 2" × 4" stock and installing insulation between the studs before you apply the panels. You will have to do some fancy widening of the window sills and frames, but you may also be able to reduce your heating bill.

Fitting Wallboard Over an Electrical Box.
When you are about to install a panel over an
electrical box, remove the outlet or switch plate
and paint the edge of the electrical box with lipstick. Then place the panel in its proper position
and press it against the electrical box. The lipstick
will imprint the outline of the box on the back of
the panel, giving you a cutting line.

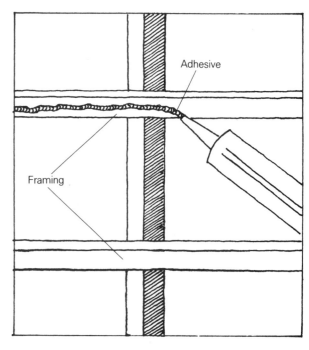

**A lipstick imprint of the outline of an
electrical box will provide an accurate
cutting line on the wallboard panel. When
positioning the panels, be sure that each
one butts tightly against the panels adjacent to it.**

**The furring-strip frame is sometimes given
an application of glue before the panels are
nailed to it.**

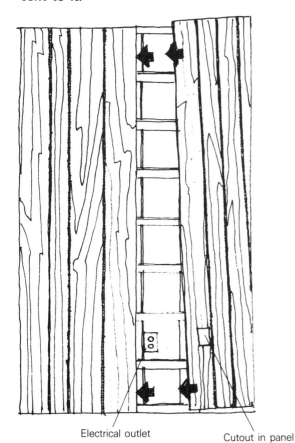

Electrical outlet   Cutout in panel

BRICK WALLS

Brownstoners are those people who buy old
urban houses and renovate them. A surprising
number of brownstoners have the notion that it
would really be sexy to expose the brick walls of
their houses, so a great many of them are prone
to removing the plaster on the walls. What they
find, after days of hard labor scraping off every
bit of plaster, is that the bricks are not very pretty,
and often need repointing. And so these brownstoners go about the arduous task of cleaning out
the mortar between the bricks and then take
weeks, even months (or spend a lot of money hiring a bricklayer) to fill in the joints with fresh
mortar.

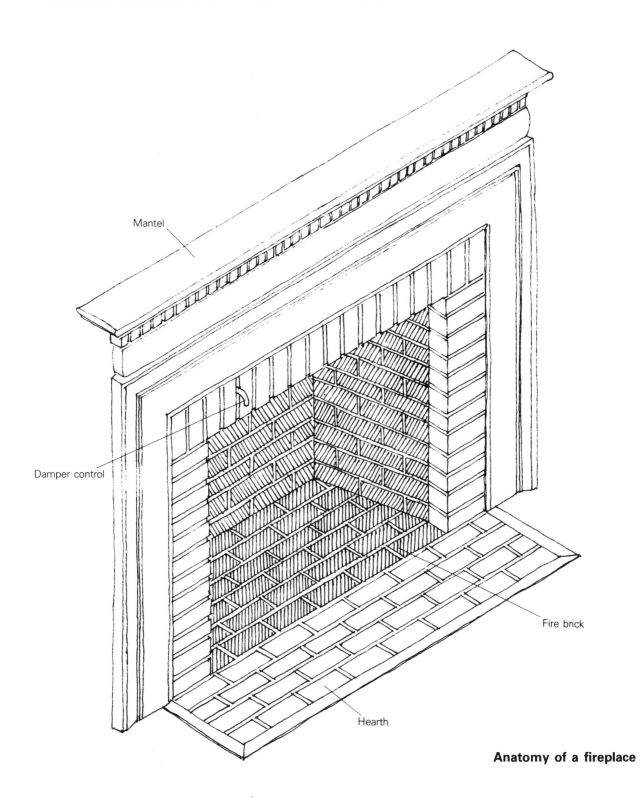

Anatomy of a fireplace

Then the wall may look gorgeous. But it won't keep the heat in. Brick is a very porous material; warm air whizzes through it as if the wall had never even been built. And the faster the warm air goes out, the more expensive it is to heat the building. If you insist on baring your brick walls, at least coat them with two or three applications of polyurethane to plug up the pores. You can use a matte finish that will not be glossy, or you can buy one of the several brick-sealing products on the market. You'll never regret the few hours' work it takes to seal the wall.

FIREPLACES

Many old houses were built with a fireplace in every room. The fireplaces were used as sources of heat for the building, as well as for decoration. Most old homes have long since had their chimney flues sealed off, and typical urban building codes now demand that any flue reopened for use must be lined with flue pipe. The notion is that the brick and mortar, as it approaches its 100th-plus birthday, has crumbled in places and weakened to a point where the chimney is now a fire hazard. If you want to reopen your chimneys, check with your local building code to determine what must be done with what materials. Also, check the cost of hiring a competent professional to do the work. Opening chimney flues can be expensive and difficult, and may not be worth the cost; as a rule, even the hardiest do-it-yourselfer will shy away from taking on flue lining as a project.

Removing a fireplace, however, is easy. Whether the mantel is made of wood or marble, it will come apart with remarkable ease. The stone mantels are made up of separate pieces cut and fitted together like a jigsaw puzzle, and are held in place by small wires and plaster of paris. If you start prying the side pieces away from the wall, you will quickly be able to see how each section is tied into the chimney. The mantel may or may not be removable before the sides are taken down, depending on whether its back edge has been buried deep in the plaster.

With the mantel out of your way, you can try to pry up the hearth stone, which, in the majority of cases, is sitting on a basket of bricks built between the floor joists. If you are trying to get rid of the fireplace, you'll have to pull the hearth out of the floor so the hole can be covered with floor boards. You can leave the brick basket buried where it is.

The fireplace opening can be sealed with a brick wall, or covered with wallboard. If you're planning to use the wallboard, stuff the hole with insulation before you cover it. The wallboard panels can, according to their manufacturers, be "glued" to a masonry wall by coating the bricks with globs of joint compound and then bracing the panel in place until the compound dries. Why not? That marble mantel was held in place for a century by dollops of plaster of paris.

Use a block as leverage when you pry the mantel of a fireplace out of the plaster.

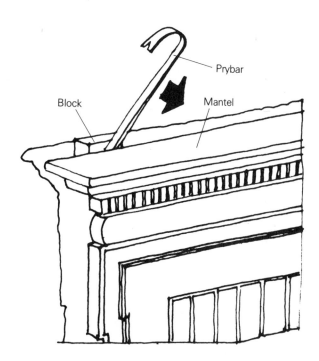

FLOORS

Everybody uses polyurethane on their wooden floors these days, and there really aren't any viable alternatives. Polyurethane is durable, easy to clean, and requires only that you sand each coat after it has dried and before the next coat is applied. Flooring should have at least two coats, preferably three; if the floors haven't been treated in the past ten years, four or more coats are ideal. Each coat must be hand-sanded with a fine-grit abrasive and then covered with the next coat. Staining, of course, must be done before the polyurethane is put down, and professionals recommend that no matter what kind of wood the floor is, it should be given a coat of sander-filler.

PARQUET

You can make your own parquet flooring from oak strips that are sold at most lumberyards, or by using oak squares. The squares are composed of six or eight wood strips held together by a paper or net backing, and usually measure 12" square. You can do all kinds of things with oak squares, such as cut them in quarters to make smaller squares, or break the pieces apart and reassemble them in, say, a swirl pattern. You can use the 2"-wide strips as borders, or dividers, or whatever you wish.

You can also buy innumerable types of squares at hardwood supplier outlets. Floor squares are made from any number of exotic hardwoods, and may or may not be already finished. The squares usually require an application of mastic to their undersides before they are placed over underlayment, but some types come with mastic already on their backs.

The most important element to laying any parquet floor is its underlayment. The underlayment must be smooth and even, and firmly nailed to the existing floor, with annular-ring flooring nails driven through it every 4" to 6" in all directions. If you are worried about the mastic drying out and the squares loosening or developing a squeak, you can nail the squares, or even each individual board in them. But remember that you are dealing with hardwood, which, if it doesn't bend your nails, will certainly split. So you must drill pilot holes for each nail. And if you are nailing the boards, try to make the nails as regular and even-spaced as you can; even if you cover them over, the wood filler will show up as small round dots.

Lay the squares out on the floor before you begin gluing them down, to be sure you have figured your pattern correctly.

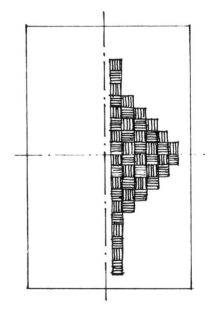

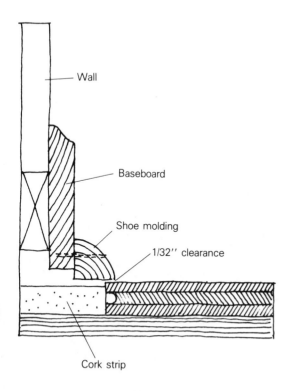

Wall

Baseboard

Shoe molding

1/32″ clearance

Cork strip

Cork expansion stripping is not absolutely necessary. But do not nail the shoe molding to the flooring, or it will split when the boards expand.

When you lay a parquet floor, try to get full squares around the doors, where the traffic will be heaviest. So begin laying the tiles from the doorways in. Even if you do not take off the baseboards in the room, plan to nail a shoe molding over the edge of the parquet. The parquet should end about a quarter-inch from the baseboard to allow for expansion of the boards in humid weather. The space between the blocks and the baseboard can be filled with a strip of cork, which is then covered by the quarter-round shoe molding. When you place the shoe, slide a piece of cardboard under it, and nail it to the baseboard, *not* the floor. Then remove the cardboard, which will leave the shoe ¹/₃₂″ above the flooring, also to allow for expansion. If you do not have a

baseboard in place around the floor, the expansion strip of cork can extend from the parquets all the way to the wall, which means it would be about an inch wide.

RESILIENT FLOORING

Whether you are installing resilient squares or rolled sheet goods, such as linoleum, it is again essential that there be a firm, even underlayment. With squares, locate the center of the room and lay two lines of full tiles—one across the full length, and one across the width of the room. There will probably be a space left between the last tile in each line and the walls. Shift the rows until the distance is identical between each end of each row and the nearest wall, so that your

Lay rows of squares across both dimensions of the floor, and adjust the rows so that you have equal distances between the last full square and the walls.

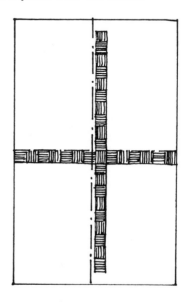

partial tiles will be equal on both sides of the room. Generally speaking, you do not want any partial tiles to be less than half the width of a full tile; to achieve that, you may have to remove one full tile from the row before you shift it.

Sheet goods can present a frightening problem in that all of the nooks and crannies of the room need to be cut out of the material before it is laid in place. You can give yourself a little leeway by planning on installing a ¾"-wide shoe molding around the perimeter of the sheet goods, which amounts to 1½" of maneuverability in both directions of the room.

The safest approach to cutting sheet goods is to take pieces of heavy paper and carefully cut them

out to fit along every part of the wall, and tape the pieces together so that you have an exact template of the floor. Then tape the paper template to the face of the sheet goods and cut it to match. If the floor is so wide that you need to lay two pieces, cut both pieces out, but leave about a 2" overlap along the seam edge. Install the sections so that they overlap each other, and then cut through both pieces at the same time using a utility knife and a straightedge. Remove the scrap pieces; the two halves should match exactly.

BOARD AND STRIP FLOORS

Houses built before World War II usually do not have subfloors. Particularly if the flooring is random-width pine planks, it has very often been nailed directly to the joists, which allows dirt and dust to sift down between the expanding and contracting floorboards and pile up on the underside of the ceiling below. Modern builders install panels of plywood or man-made material over the joists and then nail the flooring to that, which provides the advantage of a little more cleanliness, as well as structural strength. And it allows you to run your floorboards in any direction you want to if they are being nailed to a subfloor.

Without a subfloor, the floorboards must be laid at a 45° or 90° angle to the direction of the joists, and each board is nailed to every joist it crosses. Moreover, all end joints must be made over a joist. While all of that is not as critical when there is a subfloor, it is preferable that the ends of boards be nailed through the subflooring and into joists—particularly when ends are meeting.

Tradition says that narrow spaces such as closets, alcoves, and hallways, must have their floorboards running in the long direction. Tradition, in this case, comes from the fact that whoever is laying the floor will have fewer boards to cut if he lays them out lengthwise. But you can make a narrow space look considerably wider by laying the boards across widthwise, boardwalk style.

Draw right-angle guidelines on the floor before you start laying tiles, to act as your control axis.

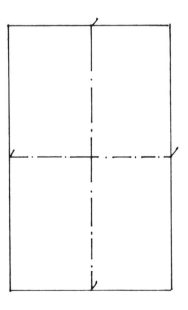

STORAGE

There is never enough storage space in any house. It tends to be nonexistent in older buildings because in bygone eras people used huge, movable closets that served as furniture as well as storage space. Consequently, a modern family moving into an old house must spend a considerable amount of time and money constructing storage space.

Closets can be carved out of a "dead" corner in just about any room, or against an entire wall, or in nooks, or to fill out alcoves. Irregular spaces can also be utilized for closet space, such as the triangle beneath a stairwell or the space between the end of a bathtub and the nearest wall. Since bathtubs are usually 5 feet long, any bathroom that is 6 feet wide or more provides an extra foot or so of room that can house shelves for storing all manner of items.

If you're planning to frame a closet, be sure to make allowances for the braces for any shelves, rods, bureaus, and racks you intend to have. It is easier and neater to make the braces for shelves or rods, for example, by adding cross members in the framing to support them, than to tack the supports on the outside of the wallboard. When you're ready to go ahead with the actual framing of the closet, the inside surfaces should be covered before the exterior side of the walls. But be sure to install whatever electrical wiring will be necessary in the frames before you cover the inside walls and ceiling.

The toilet commands a considerable amount of storage space above it, which can often be filled with shelves.

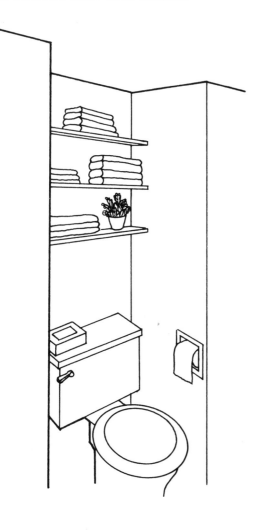

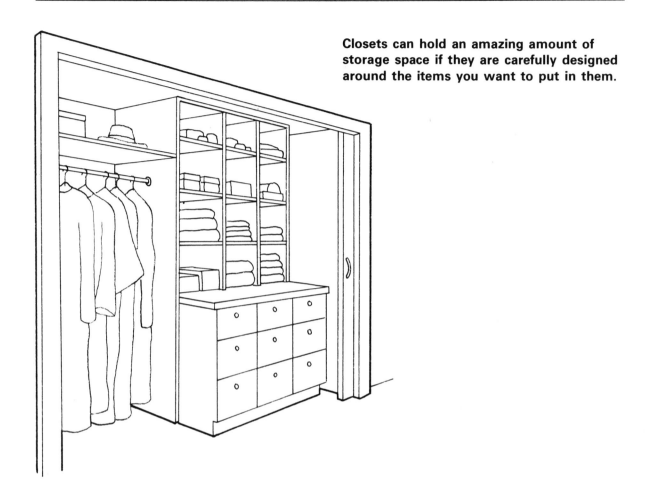

Closets can hold an amazing amount of storage space if they are carefully designed around the items you want to put in them.

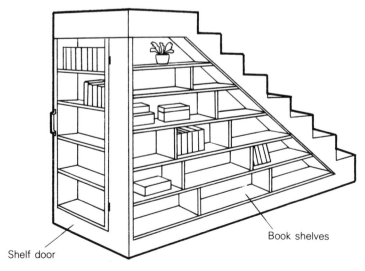

Book shelves

Shelf door

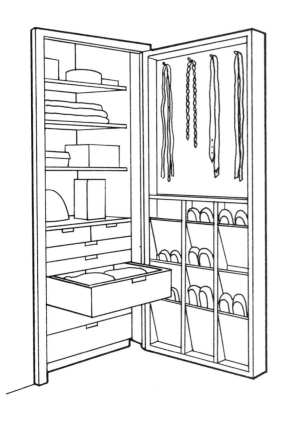

One way of making use of all the available space in a shallow closet

A "dead" corner can be filled with a ladder of shelves covered by shelf doors.

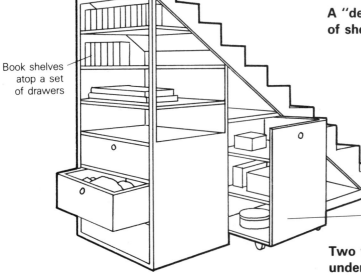

Book shelves atop a set of drawers

Roll-out shelves

Two ways of using the triangular space under a stairway

STAIRWAYS

Preponderous as they look, stairways are really not as complicated as they appear. They consist of two stringers on each side of the steps that are either notched to receive the risers and treads or have slots in them. You can buy the stringers already notched or routed, along with tread lumber (which has been milled to a curve along one edge) at most lumberyards.

Squeaky treads or risers can often be quieted by driving nails through them. The spindles, or balusters, that hold up the handrail present a different problem. If a balustrade is broken and you have all the balusters, you can glue them together with a good wood glue and put the unit back in place. If you are missing some balusters, pull one of the remaining units and take it with you to lumberyards and junk dealers; you may be able to match it exactly. If you plan to paint the balusters, you can get away with a close color match; you don't have to duplicate them exactly. Alternatively, a woodworking shop that has a lathe can turn a close resemblance of your balusters and will not charge you too much.

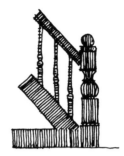

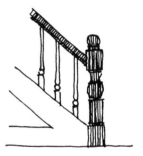

Two ways of finishing stairways: entire balustrade varnished (left); or railing varnished and balusters painted.

Some ways of getting the squeak out of a stair

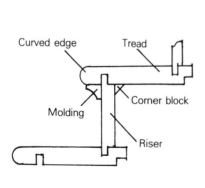

Curved edge · Tread · Corner block · Molding · Riser

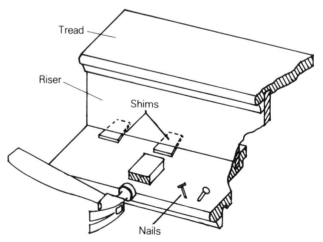

Tread · Riser · Shims · Nails

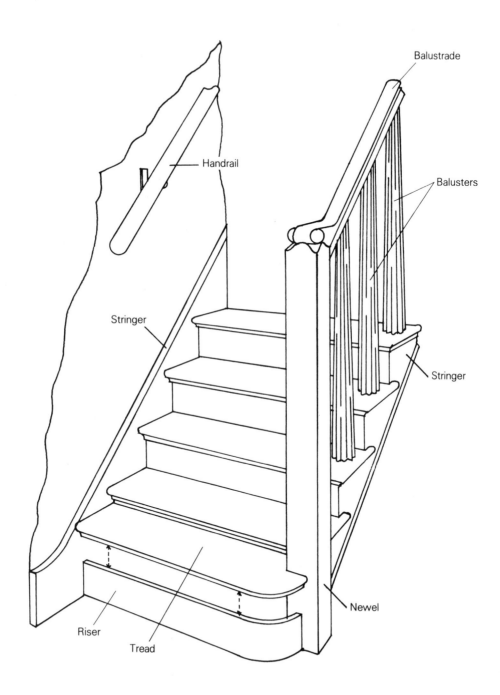

Balustrade

Handrail

Balusters

Stringer

Stringer

Newel

Riser

Tread

Anatomy of a stairway

BATHROOMS

Bathrooms rely heavily on their fixtures to key-note the decor of the entire room. Mirrors, towel bars, and decorative frames can create miracles in changing the appearance of the room. There is a whole range of different-looking fixtures to choose from, and an even wider selection of faucets that will give you everything from an antique look to a streamlined contemporary atmosphere. One interesting point about plumbing fixtures and trim: they are all made out of brass plated with chrome. You can have the chrome removed for a fraction of what it would cost you to buy gold-plated units, and the color of brass is very close to that of gold plate.

TUB SURROUNDS

One of the modern conveniences manufacturers have devised for renovating houses is the tub surround, which consists of three pieces of fiberglass or masonite that are large enough to fit over the walls behind a bathtub. The instructions that come with tub surrounds make installation sound like a dream come true compared to cutting and installing tiles, but don't believe everything you read.

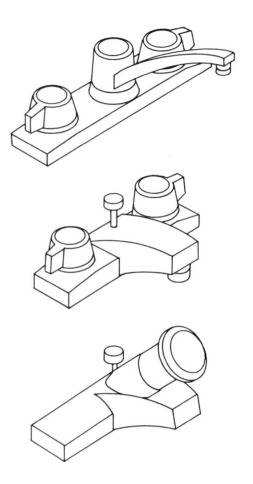

Typical bathroom faucets

How to measure the area around a tub prior to tiling

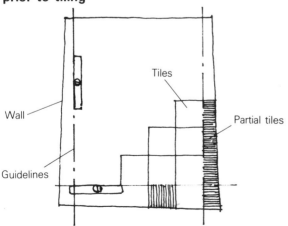

Wall

Guidelines

Tiles

Partial tiles

If the walls behind your bathtub are absolutely plumb and come together at exactly 90°, you can install any tub surround with about a day's labor. If the walls are in the least bit off plumb, you are in for some long hours of measuring and cutting and fitting and caulking, and even then you may not get the surround to form the waterproof seal that it should, particularly if you are covering an old plaster wall. If the walls are at all off plumb, tile them instead—but be sure to measure in advance. It is a whole lot easier, sometimes considerably cheaper, and definitely quicker.

6. Decorating

A SURPRISING NUMBER of people move into old houses and start their renovation by stripping all of the paint off the door and window moldings, the shutters, and even the bannisters. Given the fact that old house molding tends to be an ornate assembly of curves and ogees, flutes, grooves, and curlicues, if you are a paint stripper you are in for some long hours of tedious (and not terribly rewarding) work. And what you will probably unearth by the time you finish is a lot of cheap, not very interesting softwood that was originally made specifically to be covered with paint. You are very likely to find an uninteresting wood, but not always.

Sometimes, the molding, trim, and shutters turn out to be magnificent hardwoods—oak, mahogany, fruitwood, even rosewood. And the fool who first painted them should be punished for committing an unpardonable sin. Without question, if your molding or trim is a beautiful exotic wood, get the paint off it. Handrails are most often candidates for mahogany or some other hardwood, and so are balusters and newels. Old shutters may have hardwood panels if they are not completely hardwood, and you may find something like fruitwood panels in some of the doors. With molding and trim, you stand a 75 percent chance of encountering knotty pine or spruce.

If you want to be selective about what you strip, test each piece at various points with a chemical stripper to see what the wood looks like. If it is not worth stripping, you can paint over the spot you have cleaned. Areas to try out include any raised panels in a door or shutter, the underside of a handrail, and any corner or edge in molding.

STRIPPING

You can go out and pay $6 or $7 for a five-gallon can of chemical stripper, plus another $5 for a similar amount of cleaner, and attack your woodwork where it stands. Figure on about a year of regular part-time labor to strip all the molding, shutters, and doors in an average-sized urban row house. But there is a quicker way: lye baths.

Lye is the chemical plumbers recommend for unclogging your drains. It comes in small cans and is sold at most hardware stores and supermarkets. It is caustic, and will eat into your skin as quickly as it will the seven layers of paint on a set of shutters. In fact, if you leave the shutters in the lye bath too long, it will even dissolve the glue that holds them together.

You can make a lye bath in your bathtub, or use a metal garbage can, or build a plywood box in the backyard. Line the box with plastic sheeting (plastic is about the only material lye will not dissolve) and do your own dipping. *Never work near lye without putting on plastic gloves.* The procedure is this:

1. Fill the bath with a pint of lye mixed with each gallon of warm water.

2. Place whatever you are stripping in the bath and let it float there, occasionally turning it over or probing it with a stick to get the solution on the top surface.

3. The paint, shellac, or varnish will begin to peel and float off the piece.

4. When the piece is reasonably clean, pull it out of the bath and wash it thoroughly with clean water (a garden hose is ideal for this stage).

5. Scrub the remaining finish material off the piece with a steel brush or steel wool.

6. Allow the piece to dry thoroughly.

7. Soft woods such as fir and spruce will have a furry texture that can be sanded with a fine-grit abrasive. Some of the hardwoods experience the same roughness, and the answer in all cases is a light sanding before you apply a coat or two of finish material.

A lye bath need not be something you build yourself. You can probably find a commercial stripping company in your local yellow pages. If that fails, automotive radiator repair shops almost always have a lye bath. If you use a commercial company, whatever you give them will be back in your hands ready for sanding and refinishing in less than a week's time.

REMOVING PIECES FOR STRIPPING

A door can easily be taken out of its frame merely by pulling its hinge pins or unscrewing the hinges. Shutters are similarly easy to remove, but with shutters you are likely to have a number of them to be stripped; so the moment you take one off its hinges, mark it by scratching a number or letter, or both, in an edge of the wood to indicate which window it belongs to, and where it is placed. Get your scratching tool into the wood, not just into the paint, or the mark will not be there when the shutter comes back from its dipping. Molding and trim can also be taken off the walls, but you have to work very carefully.

The molding around doors and windows in old houses was attached with long, square nails, and often the spaces between the wood and the plaster have been filled with paint or more plaster,

making the joint reasonably tight. To get a strip of molding off a wall, run a putty knife or chisel up the crack and pry gently outward. Do this along the full length of the piece. Using the claw of your hammer and a chisel or a small pry bar, work the piece loose a few inches at a time until you can pull it away from the wall. You have to be very cautious every inch of the way to avoid splitting the wood.

The moment you have a strip of molding removed, turn it over and gently tap out all of its nails. Then scratch a marking in the back of the wood (it will most likely be unpainted) that indicates where the piece resides. You can bundle the pieces up in groups if you want to, but the chances are they will be scrambled during the process of being dipped; without markings on their backs you will spend days trying to sort them out.

If you are (very wisely) dismantling a ballustrade, the handrail may be too long for any commercial stripping company to handle. Actually, handrails are long, curved, but not complicatedly milled, pieces that can be cleaned with a chemical stripper without too much difficulty. Balusters, on the other hand, have all manner of intricate grooves, flutes, reeds, bulges, and hard-to-reach crevices that may have to be probed with a sharp tool even after they come back from a lye bath.

Each baluster is fitted into a notch cut in the edge of the stair treads and is kept from coming loose by a piece of trim nailed to the side of the tread. Pry the trim off the stair, pull the base of the baluster straight out of its notch, then yank downward to free it from the underside of the handrail. Number each baluster on its bottom (they are not necessarily all the same length), and number the tread molding if it is also going out for cleaning.

Newels are often ornate configurations made up of more than one piece of wood and may be attached to the floor, the handrail, and a stair tread or two in any number of ingenious and hidden ways. If you can get the newel out of its position, by all means have it dipped, but if removing it seems too tricky, it is only one intricate piece and you can probably suffer through stripping it by hand.

When the pieces of molding come back from their lye bath and you have sanded them, you can either put them back in place and then finish them, or finish them first. You will find that in

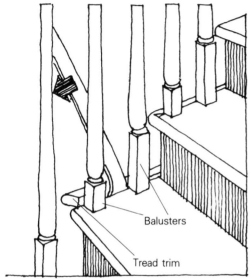

Pry off the tread trim.

Newels are often attached to the bottom steps with dadoes and grooves.

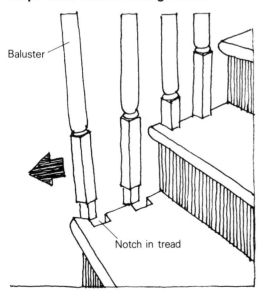

many instances you can use some of the existing nail holes in the wood, although you must choose a longer or fatter nail to rehang the molding. You can fill the unused holes and cover over all your nails with wood putty.

Heat Guns

Some of the new electrical heat guns designed for removing paint will do an excellent job of getting off much of the paint on molding, doors, and shutters, but they are not to everybody's liking. Try to borrow or rent one for a day to see how well it strips the particular items you want to clean before you go out and buy one. If you can't work with a heat gun, there is no sense wasting $30 or more for the tool; but if you can work with it, it is well worth the money.

Chemical Strippers

Sanding is not an effective way of removing paint from wood—it takes off too much wood along with the paint. So your next alternative is chemical strippers. There are dozens of commercial brands on the market, and then there are even stronger brands that can be purchased only by professionals. If you happen to know a contractor, talk him into buying some of the professional-use strippers that are available to him.

All chemical strippers are caustic and most of them will eat through your clothing and your skin, so always wear long-sleeved shirts and rubber gloves when you are working with any of them.

People usually make the mistake of buying a gallon of stripper and stretching it conservatively as far as they can. Professionals take a different approach. They practically waste their chemicals, but they can clean off all the molding and trim in a Victorian parlor in less than a day. Professionals soak about four times more area than they can expect to clean before the chemical dries. They begin scraping, stopping occasionally to soak the areas that they have yet to work on. They keep the unstripped paint wet until they get a chance

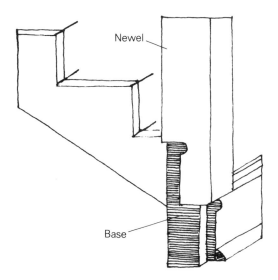

Newel

Base

Pull the baluster out of its notch in the tread.

to remove it, and as a result, by the time they reach it several applications of chemical have had a chance to soak well through the paint. Scraping at that point becomes almost nominal.

The amateur approach to paint stripping is to cover a small area with chemicals, wait about twenty minutes for the paint to curl away from the wood, scrape it off, and apply more chemical to the areas that still have paint on them. It costs less to work this way, because you use less chemical, but it takes days longer to finish the work. So the decision you have to make is, which is more important to you, your time or your money?

SOME HINTS ABOUT STRIPPING

1. Have all the right tools handy when you start work. You will need a paint scraper, putty knife, an old coffee can to hold the chemical, some cheap paint brushes (they will be eaten up by the stripper after a while), steel wool, rags or paper towels, and plenty of newspapers. For getting into crevices you'll need an awl or a nut pick, and, most useful of all, an old-fashioned, hooked beer-can opener.

2. If you are removing a clear finish, test it first with alcohol. If it is shellac or old varnish, the alcohol will do a swifter job of removing it at considerably less cost and mess.

3. Chemical strippers are sold in both a liquid and a paste form. The paste version clings to vertical surfaces without rolling, and should be used whenever you are working on a wall or any other vertical surface. The two types are equally good at removing paint.

4. Any items that can be taken down and laid flat, such as doors or shutters, will be easier to work on if they are placed on a pair of saw horses.

5. Steel wool can often be used to get into crevices and clean up stubborn areas. Scrape away as much residue as you can with a scraper or putty knife, then apply more chemical. Allow the paint time enough to pucker, then scrape it and scrub the area with a medium or coarse steel wool pad.

6. When you have removed all of the old paint, clean the wood with the proper cleaner recommended by the chemical stripper manufacturer. Many of the strippers are cleaned with water, others have their own solvent which must be purchased separately.

7. Raw wood can pick up dirt and stains very quickly. The best way to protect your stripped areas before they are given a finish coating is to stain them or apply a sander-filler, then tape plastic or paper over the entire area.

FINISHING MATERIALS

Any raw wood that is to be given a clear finish will need at least two coatings, and perhaps more. Linseed oil, varnish, shellac, and polyurethane should be rubbed down after each coat has dried, then wiped clean before the next coat is applied. You can use fine steel wool or a very fine sandpaper to smooth the surfaces. If you choose to apply polyurethane on shutters, doors, or molding, there are furniture-grade versions that provide a softer, less glossy finish than the grades of polyurethane usually used on floors.

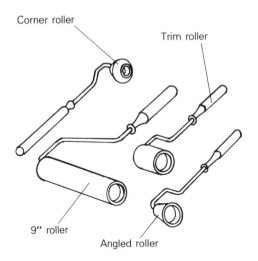

Corner roller

Trim roller

9" roller

Angled roller

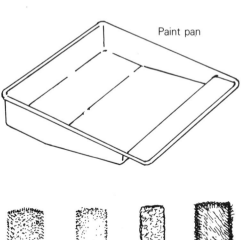

Paint pan

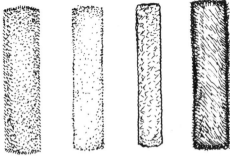

Rollers

Paint roller equipment

PAINTING ROOMS

Whether the walls are plaster or wallboard, unless they are brand new, you have a considerable amount of preparation to go through before you can start wielding your paint brushes and rollers. The cracks and holes in both plaster and wallboard can be filled with spackle or wallboard joint compound. You can buy either in powdered form, but the ready-mixed versions are easier to use.

Before you begin painting, remove all nails in the walls and take off all plates covering the electrical outlets and switches, and light fixtures. The light fixtures have escutcheons around their bases that can usually be loosened enough to paint under without taking down the whole light.

Any woodwork that is not to be painted should be protected along its edges with masking tape. If the woodwork is something like a kitchen cabinet, cover its front with newspaper or plastic sheeting and tape. Also, be sure the edges of the floor are covered and the plastic or paper covering is taped to the baseboard. Paint is tough to get off any raw wood, so cover the floor even if you intend to finish it later.

Use ready-mixed paints whenever possible. Even when your paint store is mixing according to a formula, the chances of hitting exactly the same shade in two different cans of paint mixed at different times are not very good.

Semigloss enamels should be used on woodwork. They can be acrylic or oil based, but the latex (water-solvent) enamels are just as good and are easier to work with and clean up. The finish provided by all semigloss paints tends to dull very quickly, but it is easier to clean than flat paints; you might consider using semigloss on your walls as well as the woodwork.

One of the decorative effects often used in old houses is to paint the detail portions of ceiling medallions and plaster molding a contrasting color with the rest of the units. Thus, the leaves in an ornate medallion might be painted a gold, or

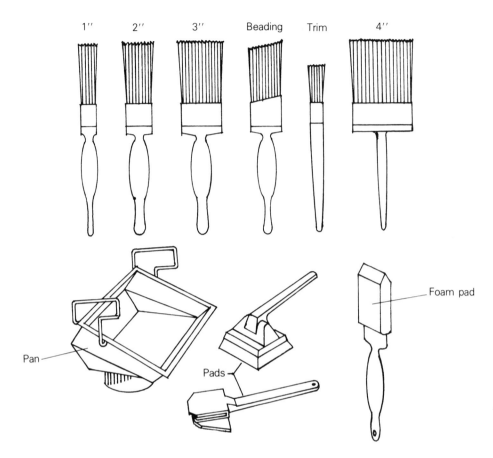

Paint brushes and painting pads

an olive green, while the rest of the unit is some other color. When you get into this kind of decorative painting, put the light colors on first, then cover them with darker colors in whatever areas are to be highlighted. Be aware, however, that going the Michaelangelo route with your crown molding and medallions is time-consuming, meticulous artistry, and you will be up on your step ladder for a long time.

LADDERS

Whether you are painting or wallpapering, if you are required to climb any ladder you are in danger of falling and hurting yourself. There are some basic rules of safety that should be observed whenever you are using ladders:

1. Make certain that the hinges on a stepladder are completely straight and locked and that all four legs are solidly on the floor.

2. Never stand higher than the third rung from the top of any ladder.

3. Don't get lazy and extend your reach when you are on a ladder. Your hips should remain inside the ladder sides.

4. Whenever possible, lay a scaffolding plank between two step ladders and work from that, rather than the ladders themselves. The plank should be clamped to the ladder rungs at both ends so that it cannot slip.

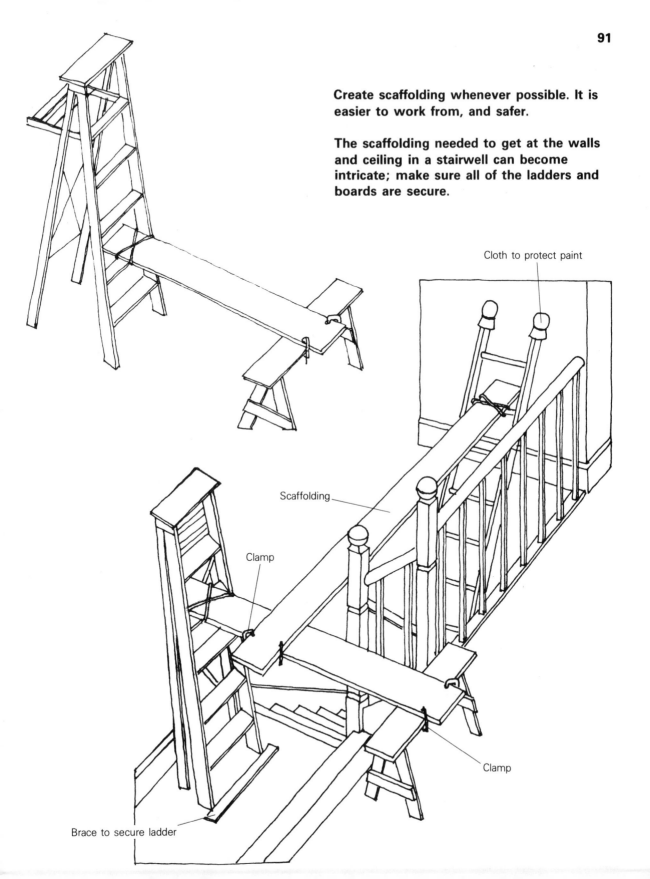

Create scaffolding whenever possible. It is easier to work from, and safer.

The scaffolding needed to get at the walls and ceiling in a stairwell can become intricate; make sure all of the ladders and boards are secure.

Cloth to protect paint

Scaffolding

Clamp

Clamp

Brace to secure ladder

WALL COVERINGS

Wall coverings used to be called wallpaper, but paper is hardly used anymore. Fabrics, vinyl, and foils are far more prevalent these days, primarily because they are tougher, easier to clean, and in many cases strippable. You can blow a mental gasket trying to pick out the right wallcovering design for a given room, because there are literally thousands of patterns and colors to choose from in any modestly sized wallcovering outlet.

Don't fool yourself into thinking that because it is the smallest room in your house, the bathroom is the easiest room to cover. Bathrooms rarely have a complete, uninterrupted wall to work with. There is always a window, or a fixture, or tile, or something interrupting the wall surfaces. What happens to people when they set about covering their bathroom walls is that they use twice as much paper as they thought they would—primarily because a tremendous amount of it is wasted working around the windows and fixtures, and trying to match the pattern. Bathrooms, by the way, experience a considerable amount of moisture everytime anyone takes a bath or shower, so the wallcovering that lasts the longest is a strippable vinyl-backed covering, preferably one with a design that does not need to be matched, or with a short pattern repeat (every 8" to 12"). Vinyl, however, is thick and the strips must be butt-seamed; it is too heavy to make overlapping seams that will not be unsightly.

Wallpapering equipment

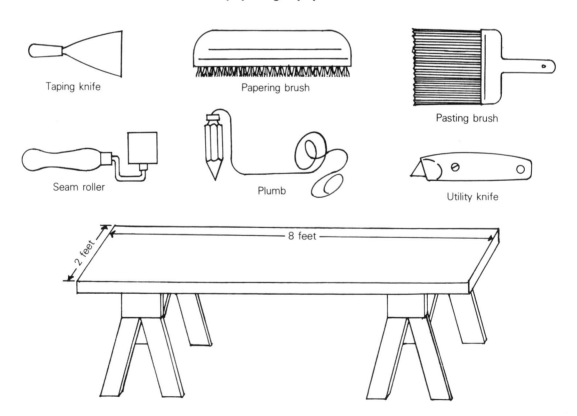

Taping knife

Papering brush

Pasting brush

Seam roller

Plumb

Utility knife

2 feet

8 feet

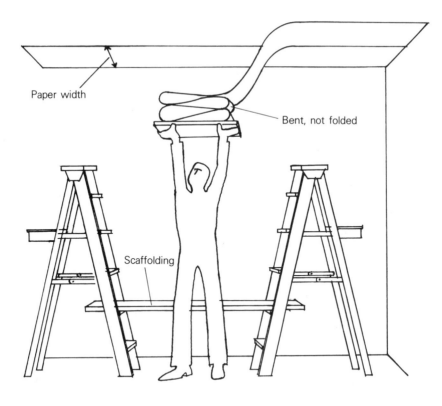

Paper width

Bent, not folded

Scaffolding

**Whether wallpapering or painting, always
start with the ceiling.**

If you have never wallpapered anything before, start your on-the-job training in a bedroom or even the living room, where you can work on full-height, uninterrupted walls. You can save an unbelievable amount of wasted covering by alternatively cutting your strips from two rolls at a time and matching them before they are put on the wall.

Some wallcoverings are sold as prepasted paper. This means the paste is already on the back of the covering and needs only to be dampened before it is applied to the walls. Prepasted wallcoverings may sound like a marketing gambit, but the fact is that many of them are much easier to use and a lot quicker to apply, since the several steps involved in mixing and applying paste are eliminated.

If you buy unpasted wallcoverings, the professionals say you are supposed to put the paste you mix on the back of the paper. But it is easier to apply it to the wall. You can paint the wall with enough paste to hold three or four strips of covering; and if the strips have already been matched and cut, you can get them in place long before the paste dries out.

No matter what the wallcovering manufacturer or salesperson tells you, coating any wall with sizing will help the paper to adhere for years to come by providing a durable glue base.

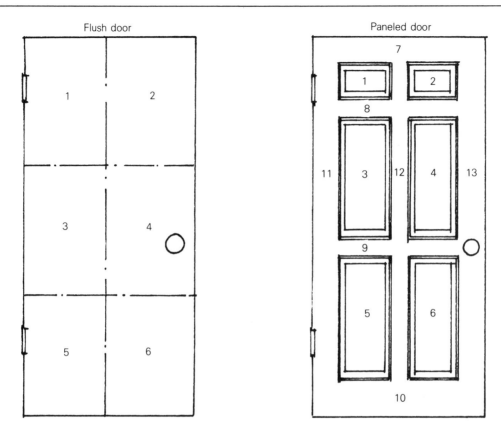

**The numbered procedures for painting a
flush door and a paneled door.**

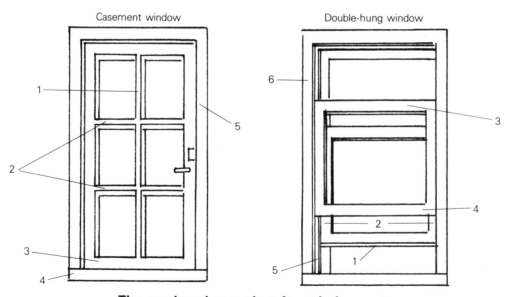

**The numbered procedure for painting parts
of a window**

PROCEDURE FOR COVERING A ROOM

Whether you are painting or wallpapering any room, there is a specific procedure that should be followed. If you are doing both, paint first.

1. Always cover the ceiling first. Protect the floor with newspaper or plastic sheeting and don't touch the walls until the ceiling is completely finished. It is infinitely easier to work on a ceiling if you set up a scaffolding, rather than use separate ladders.

2. If the crown molding and medallions are to be painted a different color, do them next. If the color is darker than either the ceiling or the walls, be careful not to slop paint on any lighter surface or it will be hard to cover up.

3. Do the walls.

4. Paint or varnish the molding and baseboards.

5. Paint the windows and doors.

6. Finish the floor last. The one variation in this procedure occurs when the floor has not been sanded. The sanding should at least be done before any painting goes on any of the other surfaces in the room, since dust will get all over everything. Having sanded the floor, you may want to put the finishing coats, or some of them at least, on the floor before you paint anything else. If the wood has a couple of coats of polyurethane on it, paint splatters will be easier to clean up than if the wood is raw.

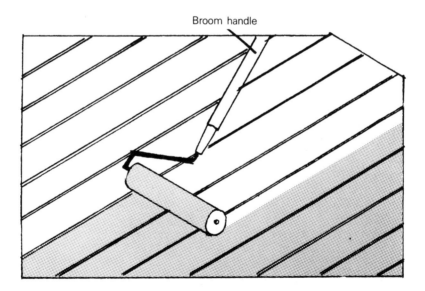

Broom handle

Polyurethane can be applied to a floor with a roller as well as with a brush.

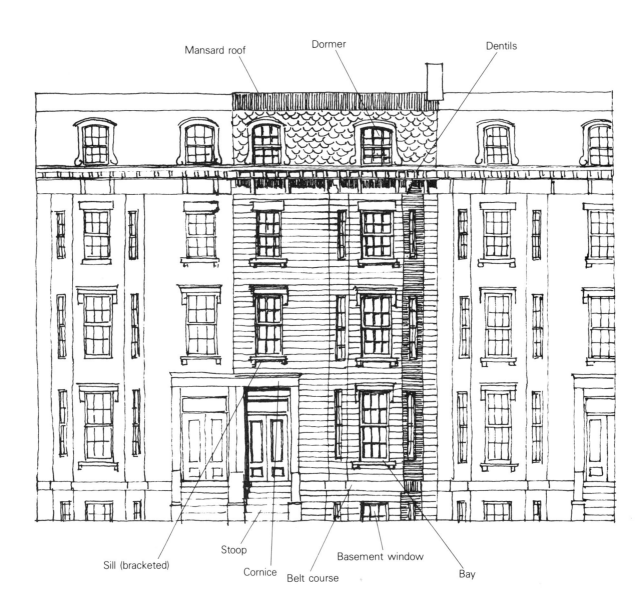

The facade of an urban row house.

7. The Exterior

THERE ARE OCCASIONS when the facade of a house is in such disrepair that the building is an eyesore to the neighborhood around it. There may be broken front steps, peeling paint, bricks badly in need of repointing, chipped concrete, bent or missing parts of an iron fence—all of which can lend to an unsightly appearance that causes your neighbors to anxiously await your exterior renovation. So neighborhood pressure can cause you to reverse normal renovation plans and attack the facade of your home before you get to building a new kitchen or second bathroom.

No matter when you turn your attention to the outside of your renovation, there are a myriad of things to consider starting with how you want the building to look when you are finished with your work, which leads to the questions of what materials you should use, and what kind of decorative effects, including colors, will be presented to the world as it passes by your front door.

MATERIALS

There are all manner of building materials to choose from but they can be divided into three broad categories:

1. The traditional, "real" materials such as brick, stone, wood, clapboard, slate, tile, and asphalt shingles. Asphalt shingles are not really traditional, but they are capable of matching in color both slate and tile and will withstand the weather almost as well as real materials. So asphalt shingles are a reasonably priced alternative to both slate and tile.

2. Materials that are acceptable when you are updating, that is modernizing, the front of a house. These include all the traditional materials plus such items as vinyl, aluminum, or steel siding, and metal window frames as well as doors constructed from energy-efficient man-made materials (providing they look like wooden units).

3. Materials that are "copies" of the traditional materials. These tend to come in outlandish col-

The Queen Anne style, dating from 1880

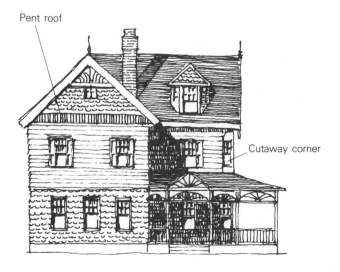

Pent roof

Cutaway corner

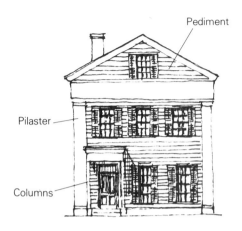

Greek Revival style, c. 1830

The Italianate, or Bracketed, style came into popularity around 1845.

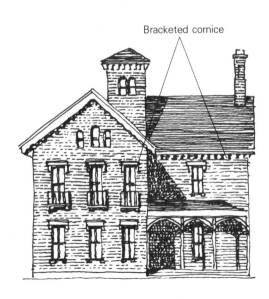

ors, and are usually unacceptable in any form. Unfortunately, this category includes an almost endless range of cheap reproductions like artificial brick or stone, asbestos shingles, and any door or window distinguished by imitation historical details, too much colored plastic, or raw exposed metal.

In general, you can assume that nothing will look better on any house, but especially an old one, than the original materials used to construct it. That means wood, brick, stone, and metal in their original colors.

RELATING TO THE NEIGHBORHOOD

In urban areas especially, it is important that your house relates to the street or neighborhood where it stands. Relating is important only because any house belongs not just to its owners, but to its immediate environment as well. At the time most of the older homes in America were built, it was considered architectural good manners to design and build residences that were harmonious with their surroundings. This did not mean that all houses on a given city block looked exactly alike. To be sure, there might be as many as a score of different facades on the same street, but if you walk down any "old" neighborhood in any city and take note of the buildings, you will notice that there is, in most instances, a harmony about their design.

The designs may be in harmony, but sometimes rehabilitation of the buildings has gotten away from the tone and character of the neighborhood, either through ignorance or egocentricity on the part of some of the homeowners. When you set about renovating an old house, particularly if it stands in an urban neighborhood, first consider:

1. Can the renovation be made with materials that predominate in the neighborhood? If all the houses on your street are brick, don't cover yours with shingles or clapboard.

Mansard roof

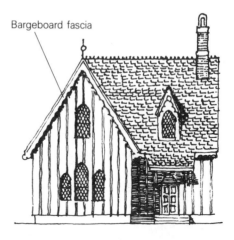

Bargeboard fascia

The Mansard style began around 1855 and is sometimes known as French Second Empire.

The Greek Revival style, with its bargeboard fascia, began about 1830.

Until World War II, it was considered architectural good manners to blend compatible designs on the same street.

2. Try to relate to the predominant textures in the neighborhood. If the brickwork is rough, use rough brickwork; if the clapboard is narrow, try to have closely spaced clapboard.

3. Use the colors that predominate the neighborhood. Don't paint your brickwork purple when everybody else uses terra-cotta or brick-red colors; leave your clapboard white or off-white like everybody else's, and suppress your desire for a day-glo pink facade.

4. Try to be consistent with the predominate details in the neighborhood. Keep the door trim, window molding, lintels, chimneys, ironwork, and so on, in keeping with the houses around you.

You can simplify a facade in the name of modernization, but try to keep all of the basic architectural elements in proportion to the original.

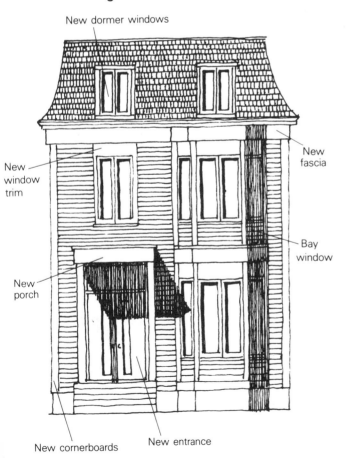

New dormer windows

New window trim

New porch

New cornerboards

New entrance

New fascia

Bay window

5. If you are adding to your building, repeat architectural elements that are already represented in the neighborhood, such as bays (rather than picture windows), and entrance ways (rather than porches). Don't put up a brightly colored fiberglass awning over the ground-floor windows if you are the only one on the block to have one. It will look more ridiculous than it really is.

6. Keep the roof line in relation to its neighbors'. If the neighborhood has low-pitched, flat, or gabled roofs, don't go hanging a mansard, gambrel, or hipped cap on your castle.

7. Keep the landscaping features in tune with your neighbors'. If everybody has wrought iron or brick fences, skip your secret urge to have a pastel-colored cement-block wall and cobblestone walkway.

BRICKWORK

Brick happens to be one of the most durable and maintenance-free of all building materials. Furthermore, the color of brick gains a richness with age that is practically impossible to duplicate. Over the years people have gotten the notion that the best way to minimize maintenance costs and increase the longevity of a brick wall is to paint it, or cover it with something like concrete. But once the brick has been covered by practically anything, the maintenance costs will surely go up.

The two most common maintenance tasks that occur with brick are cleaning and repointing. Cleaning can be done by either washing the brick with a chemical solution such as muriatic acid, or sandblasting. Sandblasting is expensive since special equipment must be used, and therefore you have to hire a contractor. You would only sandblast if the brick has deep stains or is covered with paint that is in an advanced stage of peeling. The scouring of a brick wall with muriatic acid can be done by anyone possessing a wire brush and a lot of stamina. You might find that you can do some of your rubbing with a broken brick as well as the brush.

Repointing a brick wall consists of first cleaning out all of the loose mortar in all of the joints between all of the bricks to a depth of about half an inch, and then filling the holes with fresh mortar which is then jointed to look like the rest of the original joints. It is a tiresome, time-consuming chore that you may want to hire a mason for. A professional will cost about as much as a coverup paint job, but the difference is that repointing will last for another five decades while a paint job will have to be renewed every few years.

Mortar joints in an existing brick wall can be any of more than a half-dozen types. The joints that have not disintegrated should be examined closely to determine what they are and then duplicated in the new mortar. One of the most common mistakes made when repointing a brick wall is to forget to match the color of the old mortar. It is possible to clean old bricks and even replace some of them with new bricks that are very close in color. But if the old mortar is a dark color, fresh white mortar will stand out as a frame around each of the bricks, creating the disjointed appearance of individual bricks floating by themselves apart from all of their neighbors. The problem of color, size, and design of the mortar joints is therefore a critical one, particularly if you are trying to redefine or match the original character

Mortar joints can be made with any tool that will shape the mortar the way you want it. A piece of ⅜'' pipe does nicely for making either the grapevine or the concave joints, for example.

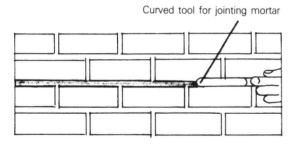

Curved tool for jointing mortar

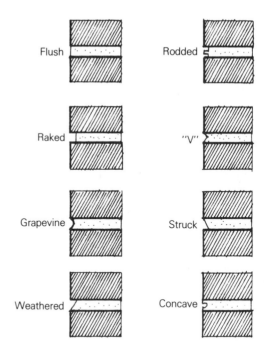

Eight of the most common mortar joints

of the wall. Usually, the solution to protecting the overall appearance of the wall is to use a dark-colored mortar so that the wall is emphasized, and not the individual bricks.

PAINTING BRICK

If the brick is one of those awkward yellow colors that is not only dingy but refuses to harmonize with anything, or if the texture of the brick is really ugly, you can either cover it up or paint it. Covering a brick facade can be as expensive as building a new wall, and most of the materials available for covering brick look infinitely worse than the brick itself.

If you decide to paint any brick walls, be prepared to maintain them—that is, repaint them every five years or so. And don't decide to be "different" and throw on some gaudy color that does not in anyway blend with the other houses on the block. Stay in the natural-color range and use shades like brick red, terra cotta, beige, black, white, or perhaps a very warm gray.

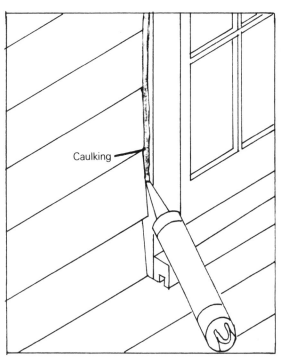

No matter what siding you install, all joints must be caulked around the windows, doors, and corner boards.

Caulking

A damaged portion of clapboard can be sawed out with a backsaw, then split with a chisel and removed.

Cut a new piece of siding to fit in the damaged area and tap it in place using a scrap of wood, then nail the piece in place.

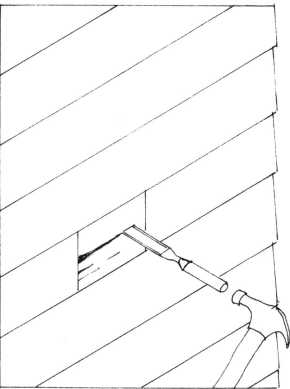

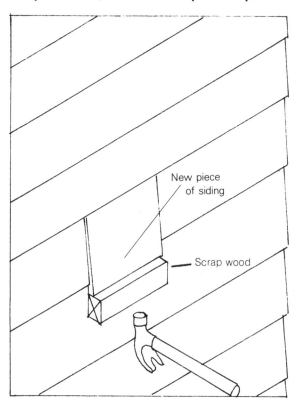

New piece of siding

Scrap wood

CLAPBOARD

Clapboard is probably the most common of all residence siding and has been used on homes for centuries. Until recently, the only clapboard in existence was made out of wood, which eventually rots or splits, and most certainly must be painted every few years. But now we have vinyl, aluminum, and steel clapboard. The synthetic clapboards have gotten pretty close to the look of wood. In fact, the manufacturers have overdone it in some cases by molding an imitation wood grain into the surface of their product; most wooden clapboard is made from straight-grained, clear pine and even with age it rarely ever shows its grain.

If you are an absolute purist dedicated to rehabilitating your home to its original appearance in every detail, use wooden clapboard for whatever repairs or replacements you have to make. But if energy conservation and a minimum of maintenance is of primary concern, take a good look at the imitation clapboard. Some of it comes with insulation glued to its back, none of it requires much—if any—maintenance, and all of it looks pretty much like the real McCoy. The vinyl siding can cost more than aluminum, but it resists denting better and its color is an integral part of the material, so it will not scratch or wear off. Steel siding is the best, and most expensive, of all. Its color is baked on the metal, it will not dent, and it has the durability of your standard neighborhood steel I-beam. When you go shopping for a synthetic siding, bear several points in mind:

1. The material, whatever it is, must look and act like real, wooden clapboard. There should be no "wood graining," for example.

2. Find a product that has the same width as the clapboard you are replacing. If you apply a wider clapboard to an old house you will subtly, but very definitely, change the scale of the building and its general appearance. Be particularly aware of the spacing between horizontal lines of the clapboard if you are only redoing part of the

exterior and are trying to match a wall or two that will continue to bear the original siding.

3. Take a look at the corners of your house. The chances are the vertical boards that cover each corner are very wide, much wider than the 2" corner trim that is typical with the synthetic clapboard. You will again change the look of the house by using a narrower corner trim, so either get synthetic corner trim that is the same width as the original, or use new wood of the proper width to go around the corners.

4. Use the existing trim around windows and doors, unless the synthetics can provide you with an exact duplication. Door and window trim is even more critical to maintaining the appearance of a building than the width of the siding or the corner trim.

Many of the synthetic sidings come with an insulation on their backs; new siding can often be installed over the existing siding.

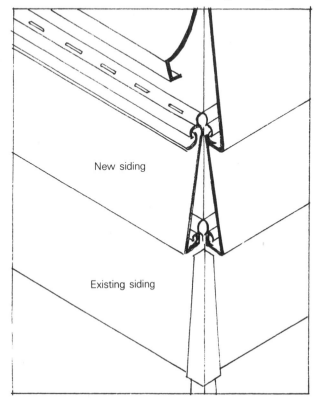

New siding

Existing siding

Don't change the width of the siding when you replace the old clapboard, or you will change the appearance of the building.

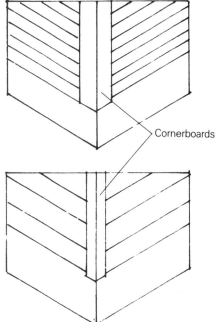

Cornerboards

Keep the width of the corner boards the same.

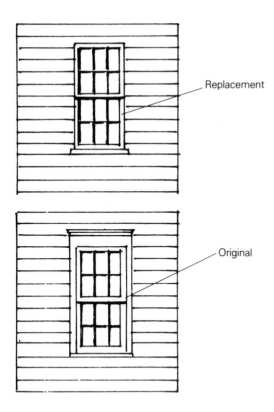

Replacement

Original

The proportion and design of replacement windows and trim should be similar to the old windows.

You cannot change clapboard to shingles without altering the entire appearance of the building—usually for the worse.

SHINGLES

Asphalt and asbestos shingles are, of course, always replacements for whatever has been on the sides of a house. But anytime you apply them to a building that has had clapboard or even wooden shingles, the look of the building is likely to change dramatically: a building that once had its facade characterized by the horizontal lines of clapboard would take on an overall texture of repetitive units that present no strong horizontal direction. The visual result would be that doors and windows that used to be an integral part of the appearance would seem to be floating aimlessly.

This is also true if you use wooden shingles or shakes in place of clapboard, although in their own right on buildings that were originally designed to be protected by them, wooden shingles are a durable, attractive covering for house walls and roofs.

Asphalt shingles, metal or vinyl clapboard, and wooden shingles can each be installed over an existing siding, provided they are given furring-strip spaces under them to hold them in place. But the thickness of the siding plus the ¾" furring strips will position the new siding out ahead of the trim around the doors and windows. So the trim must be either shimmed or replaced so that it can join to the new surface.

overall effect of changing materials in a facade is that a three-story house might have bricks around the first floor, shingles covering the second, and perhaps vertical clapboard on the third story, plus the stonework of the basement walls and whatever is on the roof. The result is three evenly divided areas, each with a different texture, one smaller section around the base of the house and still another effect above the top floor—all of which creates a very busy look. It would be considerably more restful to the eye if there were only the basement texture, a single type of siding such as clapboard or shingles, and then the roof.

If you decide that it is desirable to visually divide the floors of your house with different materials, where you put the **tide line,** or division, is

Don't get fancy about changing siding materials with every floor of the house. The building will begin to look like a parquet floor.

Most houses were designed to be covered with one type of siding, and that's all.

DIFFERENT TEXTURES FOR DIFFERENT STORIES

Many wooden nineteenth-century houses were designed and built with an elaborate use of different materials to cover various parts of the building. Some of these effects, particularly in the so called Queen Anne style, even included both vertical and horizontal clapboard directional change on the same wall. But architects today shy away from this kind of directional change except in larger areas, such as whole stories. The

extremely important. Generally, the division between exterior materials should represent what is happening inside the house. In other words, the interior of the house is divided horizontally by its floors, so it is the floors that suggest about where the exterior tide line ought to reside. You can make your division exactly where the floors are, or you can move it up or down a little. If, for example, the tide line is just under the second-story windows, the house will look as if it is sitting on a substantial, even, bulky-bottom floor. Conversely, if the tide line is moved down to just above the tops of the ground-floor windows and doors, the upper story will appear to be much higher than it really is, i.e., sitting squarely on a smaller ground floor.

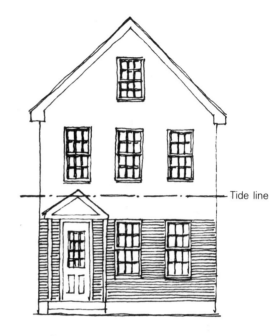

Tide line

The bottom-floor siding can be carried up as far as the second-story windows.

The top-floor siding can be brought down to the top of the ground-floor windows and doors.

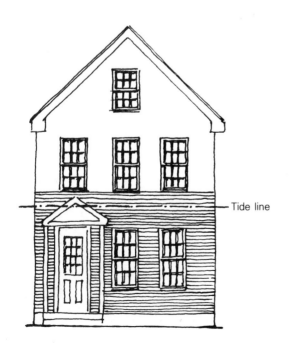

Tide line

In either case, the emphasis in the look of the building is on a horizontal division, which is not always appropriate when you are renovating many nineteenth-century houses, simply because they were often built more vertically in nature. Think carefully about making any divisions in the exterior of your old house with contrasting materials unless such a division was part of the original design.

EXTERIOR DETAILS

The facades of nineteenth-century houses are usually laden with all kinds of details such as lintels over the doors and windows, fascias, aperture trim, bay windows, and porches. But a hundred years after those buildings were first constructed, a new owner may discover some of the detail work is beyond repair and must be removed, or that someone has already removed all or part of it. If you take off all of the detail work on the front of an old house, you will arrive at a building that looks like a chicken stripped of its

The typical nineteenth-century house has a lot of architectural detail work all over its facade, all of which is absolutely in keeping with the design of the building.

You can overdo the trend to modern design and wind up with a pretty uninteresting facade.

feathers. On the other hand, finding replacement stonework or metalwork for an ailing facade can be expensive and even impossible, since the more ornate components simply are no longer manufactured.

If you go too far with your renovation of a facade you can end up with a pseudo-modernistic, very bland house front. If you take off the original detail and try to replace it with something totally different, you will end up with an unreal attempt at whatever architectural period you are trying to recreate, unless you approach the changes with a great deal of design skill—something almost no amateurs and very few professionals really possess.

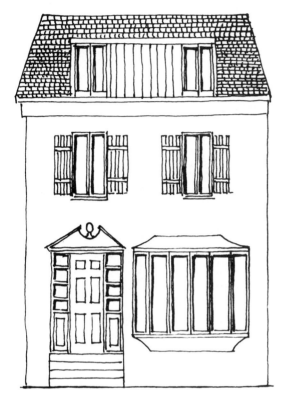

You can go halfway with a facade, with a little bit of the old and sort of some of the new, and come out with a mongrel.

Your only real recourse is to cautiously replace the missing details with simpler units that basically have the same dimensions as what has been removed. Thus, a corner board ought be the same width as the old corner boards, and the clapboards should have the same spacing, even if they do happen to be made out of fiberglass. Where the decorative cornice has been removed, you can replace it with a fascia board that is as close to the old bulk as you can get. If all or most of the stoop or porch must be taken down, construct a new stoop out of compatible natural materials and make sure that it offers the same weight to the visual appearance of the house. Don't, for example, take down 6"-wide pillars and replace them with filigreed ironwork. The

iron may be every bit as capable of holding up the roof, but it will look too flimsy for the rest of the house. If your slate roof must be replaced, don't use wooden shingles, but choose a dark-gray asphalt tile that, from the street at least, gives the same overall appearance as slate.

The idea is to replace your details with similar, if not simpler materials that provide the same bulk to the overall design of the building. Don't think of details as isolated pieces of stone or wooden fluff tacked on the front of the building. Consider them as integrated units that all work together to form a specific look to the building. If their proportions are changed dramatically, so will be the look of the whole house.

When replacing details, use materials that are compatible with the overall design of the building.

WINDOWS

Windows are the eyes of a house, and their brows are the lintels. The shadows around the eye and the eyelids become the sills, trim, and molding. If you change the windows, make sure that the attending decorative pieces maintain not only the look of the windows, but the character of the whole facade as well.

In general, you would be well advised to retain the double-hung windows that may be currently on the house, although the number of panes in each sash can be reduced, to afford the advantage of easier cleaning and maintenance. The only reason people had twelve-over-twelve or eight-over-eight sashes is that at the time the original windows were being made, technology had not developed strong enough glass to span larger areas. But by the second half of the nineteenth century, one-over-one and two-over-two windows, with their improved visibility and cleanability, were widely in use. For some reason known only to themselves, modern builders have gotten into the habit of thinking that installing six-over-six or eight-over-eight windows brings instant authenticity to whatever building they are installed in. And so they do—if the house was erected in the eighteenth century.

SELECTING REPLACEMENT WINDOWS

When you set about buying replacement windows, keep these points in mind:

1. Wooden sashes and frames should be given preference over aluminum or fiberglass. The wooden-framed windows made today often have vinyl thermal breaks in them, which help make the unit more energy-efficient but are unnoticeable from the outside. In any case, wood is a perfectly reasonable heat-retarding material.

2. If you insist on metal-framed windows, for the sake of appearance make sure there are no unpainted metal parts. Probably your best choices of color are white, black, or a bronze that has been baked on the metal and will not wear off.

3. One of the least expensive ways of improving energy-efficiency is to add storms in front of the existing windows. Unfortunately, not all aluminum-framed storms are colored, which naturally keeps their cost lower than the types with color baked on the metal work. If you have such a set of storms, or your budget only permits you to buy them, the metal can be painted by first treating it with a chemical etcher and then applying an epoxy paint.

4. Be sure that any storms you buy reflect the character of the windows they cover. Not only should the size of the muntins be approximately the same, but also the number of panes in each sash as well as the general color. Your intention with replacement windows or storms is to play down the window itself and make it blend in with the rest of the facade, so that it does not look like what it really is—an add-on piece of equipment.

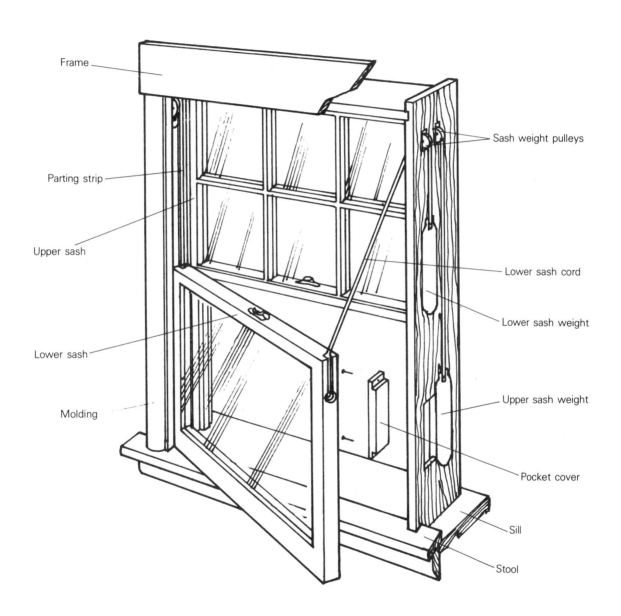

Frame

Parting strip

Upper sash

Lower sash

Molding

Sash weight pulleys

Lower sash cord

Lower sash weight

Upper sash weight

Pocket cover

Sill

Stool

Anatomy of a double-hung window

CORRECT

INCORRECT

Shutters must look as though they could close over the window they attend, even if they are nailed to the wall and can't move.

If you have a mullion between windows and can't get a shutter between them, the side shutters must look large enough to cover the glass.

Don't put tiny shutters beside a wide window. The effect does not make architectural sense.

Don't put shutters anywhere that they cannot lie flat against the wall. The result, as shown, does not look well.

INCORRECT

INCORRECT

SHUTTERS

Lots of old houses have shutters on the inside of the windows, where they can be easily operated. But just as many houses have their shutters nailed to the outside wall on either side of the windows. Newer homes in particular are likely to wind up with pasted-on shutters, primarily because builders have gotten the notion that it makes the structures look more "traditional" and confers instant respectability on the houses.

The important point about shutters is that they should look like they work, even if they don't. The plastic and metal replicas of shutters that abound on the open market today don't look like they can do anything, primarily because they look like plastic or metal replicas of wooden shutters. So they are just nailed into the siding on any side of the windows where there is space enough to hang them. And therein lies the problem. If you have a wide window with two narrow shutters on either side that would not come even close to closing off the glass, the shutters look as if they don't work. And they don't. Similarly, if you have two windows close together and there is only one shutter between them, those on the far sides of the frames won't look as if they have any function, either.

The basic question to ask when you are deciding about the shutters around your windows is simply, how much space is there for them? If there is no room between two windows for a shutter to lie flat, the two outside shutters will have to look as if they are as wide as the windows they are supposed to cover. If there is just enough room between two windows for one shutter, you can end up with what looks like a row of shutters that is occasionally interrupted by a window. With some facades that might look quite acceptable, but you can only decide that by judging for yourself.

BLOCKING UP AND BLOCKING DOWN

If you remove an old window and install a smaller one in the hole, the hole must be made smaller. You might make this change for any number of reasons: a ceiling might have been lowered so that it cuts across the top of the window, or perhaps a newly erected wall cuts into the side of the window, or the old windows are in the wrong place, or they are badly proportioned.

Blocking up or blocking down can really be done in only one way: fill in the hole with the same material used for the rest of the facade. If there is a lintel and/or a stone sill, these should be removed and replaced in their proper position above or below the aperture. All of this is not a terribly complicated procedure if the outside of the house is clapboard or shingles, or even stucco. But brick-and-stone houses present some complicated, and therefore expensive, maneuvering that might best be left in the hands of a professional. What you cannot do with any reasonable end result, although people attempt it all the time, is merely to block up the hole, particularly with a different material than that used for the rest of the wall. If you block down from the lintel, for example, you wind up with a lintel floating aimlessly in the middle of the wall. If you block up, the sill is left unattached. If you highlight your renovation by using a different building material around the window, your indiscretion will be there for every passerby to snicker at.

Trying to be symmetrical with your blocking up does not help at all, unless the siding is carried as far as the edges of the window frame.

INCORRECT

If you have to block down, fill the space with the same siding material used on the rest of the wall.

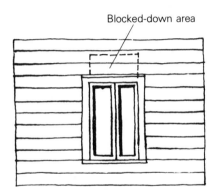

Blocked-down area

ENTRANCEWAYS AND DOORS

If the windows are a building's eyes, the front door is its mouth. More important than that analogy, a main door and the entranceway or porch around it can determine the whole character of the house. Consequently, the front door is often the first element people renovate in an effort to effect a quick change in the look of the building. Unfortunately, there is a wide selection of plastic and metal door equipment, including canopies, doorknobs, knockers, and storms, that are guaranteed to transform the appearance of your home

Most doorways are symmetrical and are often ornately appointed.

with a Saturday afternoon's labor. They will change the looks all right, but seldom for the better.

If at all possible, any changes you make to the door or entranceway during your renovation should be consistent with the remainder of the facade. You can, of course, modernize the look of a door merely by simplifying it. An ornate fanlight and side windows, for example, might be simplified to a D-shaped panel or single strip of undivided glass. Essentially, all of the changes you make, whether you are not able to find replacement units or you simply want to update the looks of the house, must be kept in the same proportions as the original.

It is even more critical to keep the symmetry. In many instances the door was originally set to one side of the porch, but the porch is often considerably larger than the entrance area. If you have a narrow entranceway or small porch, the door most likely stands in the center; if you renovate the area and place the door to one side or the other, the entire entrance will become lopsided.

The look of the entranceway or porch must be taken into account, too. Porches often fall into disrepair and become candidates for major renovation. If you cannot rehabilitate the porch to its original splendor, you still have to keep its visual impact on the face of the building well in mind. Even if you decide to eliminate the preponderance of decorative work around a porch, it still has a roof that presents a definite line over the deck and steps, and there are probably columns that were originally sized to meet the visual requirements of the building behind them.

If you are replacing the porch, keep all the new characteristics in proportion to everything you remove: keep the roof fascia as wide as it was before, maintain the same width of diameter of the posts, allow the steps the same width and height. Moreover, all of the essential parts in the original should be represented in your renovation. If there is a triangular pediment over an entablature, keep them both, in their original proportions.

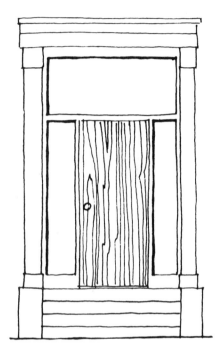

You can simplify an entranceway, but be sure to maintain its original symmetry.

A door offset in a narrow entranceway does not look well.

If there is an entablature and a pediment in the original, they should be represented in your renovation.

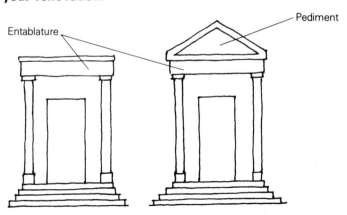

Entablature

Pediment

DORMERS

Any dormer that forms an important element in the original design of the house ought to be left alone. In Queen Anne and mansard roofs, for instance, the dormer is an integral part of the design, and you should avoid removing it, if you can. The dormer, of course, might be rotted, or it might be too small to provide proper headroom under the roof, in which cases it will have to be reconstructed. But again, try to keep the exterior elements in proportion to the elements in the original.

Adding dormers is not a difficult renovation project, but there are some considerations to look at closely:

1. Just because the dormer is high up on the roof is no reason to think it is an entity unto itself. True, the strong line of the roof seems, at first glance, to separate the dormers architecturally from the other windows in the same wall. Actual-

Dormer windows should be the same type and style as the wall windows, and also be aligned with, or proportioned to, the wall windows.

When you plunk a dormer any old place on the roof, it will stand out like a wart. This dormer should be centered over the window below it.

One way of making a large dormer is to connect two small ones with the same siding as is on the house.

A true shed dormer dominates a roof and takes as much labor and materials as creating a mansard roof.

The mansard, particularly on an old house, is a more honest statement of your intention to have more space in your top floor. And it is historical in design.

ly, the windows in a dormer should be the same type as the rest of the windows in the facade, and in the same proportion.

2. Visually, the windows in a dormer should either line up with the windows below it, or be located midway between the wall windows.

3. Problems in the proportion of dormer windows arise when you need to install an unusually large or wide dormer to provide maximum headroom in the top floor of the house. One of the ways of getting around the wide dormer problem is to space the windows in it over or between the wall windows and carry the siding up the wall between them.

4. Sometimes a dormer becomes so large that it literally takes up all or most of the roof. At this point you are basically building a whole new floor on the top of your house, which requires moving all or most of the rafters. With a relatively new home, you can get away with such an arrangement, but an older residence can look a little peculiar with an entire shed dormer stuck on its top. Many older homes will remain presentable to the world, however, if your renovation goes just a little farther and turns the roof into a mansard or gambrel and openly expresses the fact that you needed more space in the top floor and took it.

ADDITIONS AND EXTENSIONS

There are no rules to cover just how far you can depart from the original design of a house and its details during a renovation. It is not true that everything old is good. Nor is it true that everything new is bad. Furthermore, it is not true that the old and the new can never be mixed. You can, in fact, improve on an original design by judiciously carrying elements of its details and style over to a newly constructed addition or extension.

The real trick is to be definitive about what you are doing, and not wishy-washy. If you build a modern wing on the back of your house, let it stand as a wholly modern wing. If you elect to be traditional in your design, then remain faithful to the architecture of the rest of the building. But don't be a little traditional and sort of modern, and maybe kind of something else as well.

The traditional approach can present a problem at the point where it joins the main building. If you add a wing to the back of your house, for example, and make it as wide as the house itself, where it joins the house proper can become an awkward mismatch of old brick and new, or slightly different clapboard. From the standpoint of design, if you set the new structure back from the original walls you automatically have a broader range of usable materials that will not have to match up with anything old. Similarly, the details in the new structure can resemble the original details less. You can, in fact, often get away with completely different siding in a recessed addition, whereas you cannot do that very often in the middle of what amounts to a single wall surface.

Even though you are attaching a modern wing to the side of an old building, it should echo at least some of the details in the original structure. The materials in the walls and roof might be the same, for example, or the floors in both parts of

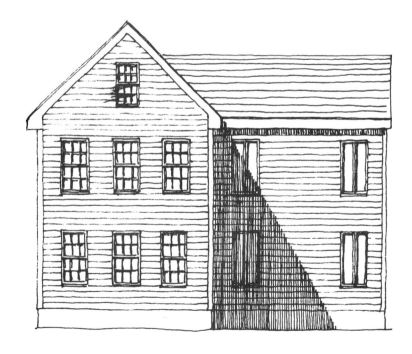

If you put a modern wing on your old house, let it stand out as modern but try to carry over some details from the original part of the building: keep the doors and windows the same proportion, for example.

the house might line up, or the vertical proportions of the windows and entranceways might be the same.

You can save yourself considerable grief by creating a definite link between the addition and the rest of the house. Such a link might be an entranceway, or perhaps a deliberate change in siding, or a different roof level. Be careful about roofs, however, when building onto an existing house. In general, keep the roof of your addition at the same pitch, or slope, as the rest of the building. Often, a flat roof can successfully be related to a pitched roof, but a single pitched roof usually does not look well with another roof that has a different angle.

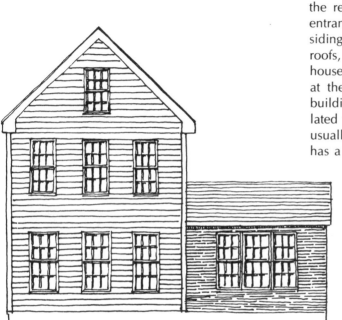

If the side of a new wing meets the side of the original house, you have to make an exact match in the siding or provide a definite division, such as with a drainpipe.

By recessing your addition, you can get away with different siding and a wider range of details that can be dramatically different from the rest of the house.

Glossary:

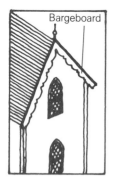

Bargeboard

Bay window

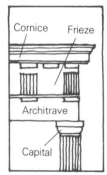

Capital

Architrave The milled trim around a door or window opening.

Bargeboard A decorated vertical board covering the ends of a pitched roof and overhanging a gable.

Bay Window A projecting bay with straight sides and windows. Bays extend to the ground on the outside of the house and therefore provide added floor space inside.

Beam Girder A large horizontal member in the cellar supported by columns or pipes, extending the length of the cellar at about the midpoint of the house width. Beams support the joists at their centers.

Belt Course A horizontal "belt" created by a course of projecting bricks or stones in a masonry wall, for decorative effect.

Bow Window A curved bay window that looks like half a tower stuck to the side of the house running from the ground to the roof.

Bracket A small projection that supports, or appears to support, a lintel or cornice.

Capital The head, or top, of a column.

Clapboard Horizontal, overlapping boards covering the outside walls of a house. On older houses the overlap is between 4″ and 6″.

Classical Architecture A type of architecture used by the ancient Romans and Greeks, and subsequent styles based on it, such as Georgian, Federal, Greek Revival, Renaissance Revival, Italianate, French Second Empire.

Clerestory Windows Windows located high in a wall, such as immediately under the roof.

Classical architecture

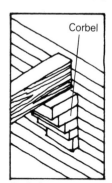

Corbel

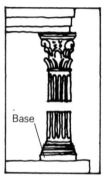

Corinthian column

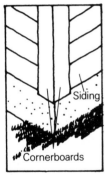

Corner board

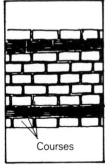

Cornice

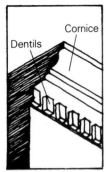

Course

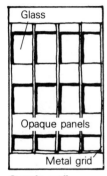

Curtain wall

Column A vertical pole or pillar supporting a roof or other structure.

Conduit The pipe used to hold electrical cable in outdoor installation. Most local building codes demand that all outdoor cable be protected from the weather by a conduit casing.

Contemporary Architecture Architectural designs and styles belonging to the same period in history.

Corbel Any projection from a masonry wall used as a decorative effect and sometimes as a support.

Corinthian Architecture One of the three basic modes of architecture established by the ancient Greeks.

Corner Boards Narrow vertical boards that cover the corners of a wood-frame house. The siding butts against the edges of the boards.

Cornice The top portion of an entablature, usually molded and projecting from the wall. Any molded transition between a wall and ceiling.

Course A row of building material, such as bricks, often positioned for decorative effect.

Curtain Wall A light, non-load-bearing, weather-proof wall placed over the face of a building. Usually this is a metal grid that contains opaque panels. Curtain walls are an inexpensive, simple way of hiding a degenerated exterior wall.

Dado The lower part of an internal wall that is divided horizontally; if the dado contains wooden panels, it is often referred to as the **wainscot.**

Dentil One of the series of horizontal blocks resembling teeth found in the lower part of a cornice or used as interior molding.

Doric Architecture One of the three basic modes of design developed by the Greeks.

Dormer A structure projecting from a pitched roof and including a window or windows.

Elevation A head-on drawing of the face of a building or part of a building, such as a wall, that does not attempt to show any perspective.

English Bond A design of bricklaying in which every other course, or row, is laid with the brick ends facing outward.

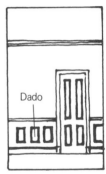

Dado

Doric column

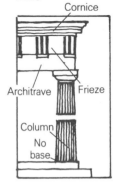

Dormer

Elevation drawing

English bond

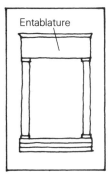

Entablature

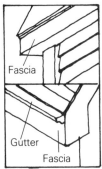

Fascia

Flemish bond

Entablature A horizontal member extending across the top of, and supported by, columns.

Fascia A flat board nailed to the ends of rafters forming at the eaves of a roof. The gutter system is often nailed to the fascia.

Flemish Bond An assembly of bricks in which every other brick in each course is installed so that its end is visible.

Gable The triangular area in the ends of a house between the eaves line and the roof peak.

Gambrel Roof A roof having two pitches to provide more headroom under the roof. Gambrel roofs have gable ends.

Half-bath Any bathroom that does not have a tub or shower.

Hipped Roof Hipped roofs have two angles, or pitched roofs, on all sides and do not contain any gable ends.

Ionic Architecture One of the three basic types of architecture developed by the Ancient Greeks.

Jamb The vertical sides of a door or window opening, typically made from ¾'' stock nailed to the aperture studs.

Joist A horizontal beam that supports a floor and/or ceiling. In older homes the joists can be anywhere from 12'' to 24'' o.c.

Leader A vertical pipe used to conduct water from the roof gutter system to the ground. Sometimes known as a **downspout**.

Lintel A horizontal beam (often stone or wood) placed in a masonry wall over doors or windows. Lintels are mainly decorative, but they will help to support the wall above the aperture.

Mansard Roof A roof having two pitches in order to provide more headroom in the top floor of the house. Mansard roofs have no gables.

Masonry Any material which is laid in small units, such as brick and stone.

Mass The effect of a solid object seen from the outside. Mass has height, width, and depth.

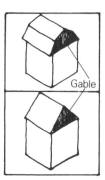

Gable roof

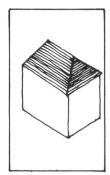

Gambrel roof

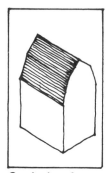

Hipped roof

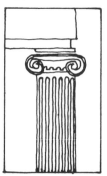

Ionic column

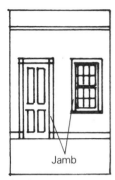

Jamb

Lintel

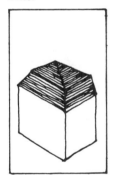

Mansard roof

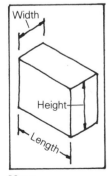

Mass

Molding A decorative band of material used in cornices and as trim around doors and windows. Outside a house, molding is likely to be made of wood or stone; inside the material is usually plaster or wood.

Muntin The horizontal and vertical strips of wood or metal that separates the panes of glass in a window.

Mullion The vertical member between windows set close together.

O.C. On center. The distance between the center of two adjacent framing members.

Order In classical architecture the order consisted of a column, or shaft, that might or might not have a base, a capital, or head, and a horizontal entablature across the top of the column. The decoration of orders was divided by the Greeks into three distinct styles, Doric, Ionic, and Corinthian. Later, the Romans added three more, The Tuscan, Roman Doric, and Composite. Still later, during the Renaissance period, there was a lot of borrowing from the Romans, so that the orders found in homes today have columns that are reminiscent of the Roman styles.

Oriel Window A projecting bay window that does not touch the ground on the outside and may not reach the floor on the inside. Often confused with bay windows.

Pane The transparent panel made of glass or plastic that forms a window. Panes are held in place by sash frames and muntins.

Partition Wall A wood-framed wall inside a house. It may be non-load-bearing or load-bearing.

Pediment A low, triangular gable in classical architecture, created by the slopes of a roof over an entablature.

Perspective Drawing A drawing of a building or its interior that conveys dimensional perspective.

Pilaster A decorative flat or half-round column that looks like it is partially embedded in a wall.

Pitch The angle of the slope of a roof.

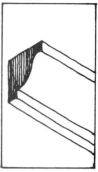

Molding

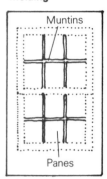

Muntins

Mullion

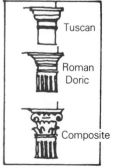

Roman orders

Oriel window

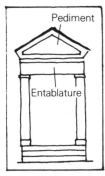

Pediment

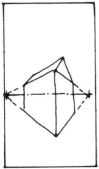

Perspective drawing

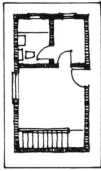

Plan

Plan A one-dimensional drawing representing a horizontal cross-section of a room or building, showing the position of walls, door, windows, stairs, etc.

Pointing The process that finishes mortar between bricks in a variety of joint configurations. Repointing means to remove about a half-inch of the mortar when it has begun to crumble, and fill the space with fresh mortar that is then given the same joint design as the rest of the wall.

Rafter One of the sloping frame members that hold up a roof. Rafters look like joists set at an angle, but they are not joists. Rafters support roofs; joists hold floors and ceilings.

Riser The vertical portion of a stair that holds up the tread.

Roof Types Roofs can be **flat** or **pitched.** The **shed roof** is a flat roof that slopes in only one direction. **Pitched roofs** can slope at any angle in two directions and have gable ends. If the pitch is continued over the ends of the house it becomes a **hipped roof. Gambrel roofs** have two pitches and gable ends. **Mansard roofs** are hipped roofs with two pitches in each of four sides.

Sash The movable portion of a window, forming the outer frame around the glass pane or panes.

Shutters Small wooden doors attached to the sides of windows, either inside or outside the house.

Siding Narrow horizontal or vertical boards attached to the outside of a house to protect it against the weather. Siding can be wooden clapboard, shingles (or shakes), or it can be made from such materials as asbestos, aluminum, asphalt, fiberglass, or steel.

Sill The lowest horizontal member in a window or door opening, constituting the bottom of its frame.

Soldier Course A horizontal row of vertically installed bricks. Usually used as a decorative feature over doors and windows.

Space The interior area of a cube. The outside of a house represents mass; the inside is space.

Structural Wall Any wall that supports part of the floor and roof load of a house. Structural walls either extend all the way to the ground or rest on the beam in the cellar.

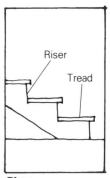

Riser

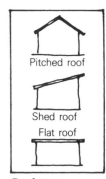

Roof types

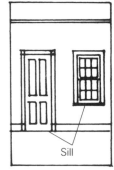

Sill

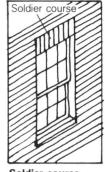

Soldier course

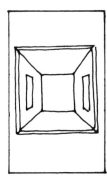

Space

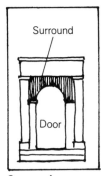

Surround

Stud Any vertical framing member in a framed wall.

Surround The molded trim around a door or window.

Tread The horizontal members of a stair, supported by a riser.

Wainscot The paneled area around the base of any interior wall. (See **Dado**)

Winder A tapered stair tread. By using several winders in a stairway you can turn it in another direction. If all of the treads are winders you have a spiral staircase.

Window Windows are **panes** of glass held in a **sash,** which slides or fits into a **frame.** The dividers between panes are called **muntins.** If two side-by-side windows are separated by a wide vertical piece of wood, the divider is known as a **mullion.**

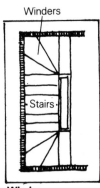

Winder

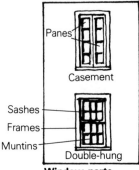

Window parts

Index